Forces...

Gangs to Riots...

Evolution to Gangs, Riots and Back to Peace

Steven David Valdivia

Volume 1

Third Edition

Dedication

To those doing it then, now and tomorrow and would heed its message. You are the spark to ignite a movement to take back communities from the gangs *and* to make fundamental changes to a system that supports their existence. I wrote this especially for the next young bucks going heart first and unreservedly into the violence maelstrom with the desire to change it...and to continue the societal changes many before you gave their lives for.

This is a smart-guide in three volumes that explains: how we got here and why we must have systemic change; the unadorned truth about the gangs and gang members; and finally a roadmap to actually begin to accomplish what others have not been able to. I wish someone had left one for me when I began in 1971. Perhaps more children would have survived. So please continue the work...ask God for strength, wisdom and guidance and go ahead and change our world.

Steven

Acknowledgements

No one accomplishes anything alone...but...

he alone decides his role

Steven D. Valdivia

For mom...

...and all God's children that she helped and will help...

This work is dedicated to God who guides my life, *and to our Mom, Eva* who raised us, taught us decency, good values and self-respect. And to my wonderful wife Bernice, (Neecee) for her Love and for standing with me during some very tough times (and Clori, Lynae and Dylan); To my courageous sister, Christina, our earliest heroine (thank you), and Howard and Stephanie for supporting her; Vincent the tough and talented businessman and Rebecca; To my big little sister Leila Renée who for as long as I can remember has done for others, changing the system along the way - and her partner in crime, Marty; Yvonne (and Megan, Anthony, Raymond & Katelyn), and Deanna (and Rianna, Elijah, Anthony, Rudy & Jocelyn) mi familia, mi corazon.

Mr. Kelly Presley who worked for all people in all things and Gene Anderson, a true revolutionary for children – two un-rewarded friends and mentors who are comfortable traveling outside any box; and Rosa Valle for timely help and encouragement.

To Eddie Olmos and Mike Farrell who see what I see and do what they do; To artist and sculptor Robert Graham who used his talent to instill hope and rebuild families; and Leo, Margaret, Viv, Alex (Moto), Olga and Nat, too; and Lonnie Wilson whose heart had room for all. And LAPD Captain Bob Ruchoft, a good and loyal friend.

Dr. Julius Griffin and Pastor Richard Matas...thank you! The Rogers family and Ray Otero who talked me into this work in the first place; And her Honor, US District Judge Marcia Cooke - our heart to heart talks prompted this next phase.

And to those whose lives were lost from birth, may you rest in peace. And to all of our children - they are why we do what we do.

CONTENTS

The Valdivia Paradigm:

Peace and violence status are relative points in time and place, are driven by many variables and emerge as periodic manifestations of historical societal processes

> *...we get there on purpose*

Gangs and other types of virulent community violence are <u>outcomes</u> of such processes...as is peace. Thus... violent outcomes are temporary, and communities can be made more peaceful... but only as a manifestation of re-formed socialization processes...

> *...we can get <u>there</u> on purpose*

Forward

I have known Steven Valdivia for many, many years. We first met when I searched him out after a spate of gang violence in the Los Angeles area resulted in a number of gang "experts" being interviewed on television. Steve was the only one who made sense to me. While the others spoke in terms of reaction, containment and control, Valdivia addressed the root problems, insisting that there were reasons for the behavior that was causing so much fear in the community. While concerned, as was everyone, with finding a solution to this problematic behavior, he insisted that without understanding and addressing the root causes, the systemic problems creating the circumstances that made what is essentially self-destructive anti-social behavior attractive to young men and women, we were attempting to put a band-aid on a gushing wound and would only condemn ourselves to a losing battle that promised further and growing warfare in the community.

Sadly, his words were prophetic.

Steven Valdivia's years-long efforts to pinpoint and articulate the fundamental issues at the root of our "gang problem" have now been condensed into a form available to us. If we hope to create a responsible and responsive society that embraces its members and deals with its problems effectively and realistically, we must open ourselves to the views of those who have had the courage to go to the source to examine the issues from a human perspective and heed them.

Some years back I heard then-President Bill Clinton address the "gang problem." As is the wont of too many so-called 'leaders,' he characterized gangs as 'the enemy' and discussed some of the ways in which we must fight them. I found myself wanting to shout, "These are our children you're talking about! Why don't we take a look at how we're failing them?" Why don't you, I thought, talk to Steve Valdivia?

Mike Farrell

I have been involved for a number of years in activities in Los Angeles as well as other parts of the country to prevent youth violence and have worked with Steven Valdivia on many of those occasions. I have read Mr. Valdivia's concept outlining the importance of examining provenance of violence elements by evolutionary phases to fully understand how violence develops is on target, and believe his new reasoning and approach goes to the fundamental building blocks of youth violence.

__Edward James Olmos__

Steven D. Valdivia is co-chair of the Peace and Non-Violence Research Group for the Institute for Computing in Humanities, Arts and Social Science (I-CHASS) at the National Center for Supercomputing Applications (NCSA), University of Illinois, Urbana Champaign.

Mr. Valdivia's work is at the interface of peace studies and cyberinfrastructure. The Research Group he co-leads explores advanced data analytics and visualization technologies applied to violent crime data repositories for knowledge discovery and to guide policy decisions by municipalities and community based organizations.

__Dr. Kevin Franklin, UIUC__

Getting to the roots of youth violence

There is another world hidden in plain sight, mirroring our own but upside down and opposite. Its birth made possible by raging hostilities, in secret and exposed. To ensure its continuation we all fight on in scaled down battles reflecting the need to maintain a war footing, guarding it as if it were a sacred right. Real blood and real guts are spilled, nonetheless. And gatekeepers hold sway until bastions are toppled one by one - but not fast enough as some are dying to tell us.

In dark places, wounded young soldiers collect their deadly inheritance fighting themselves to an early grave, for nothing short of death will do. Their self-destructive violence would seem to confirm their worthlessness, but it's their way of proving themselves finally worthy. Some are nothing less than suicidal. Their running battles a last cry for help in their mini-world of hopeless desperation, seeking a martyr's death as their last act of vengeance against sworn enemies. These soldiers, our children, share a kinship with groups from other lands and other times yet unrevealed as they go about ceaselessly imploding; a kinship by default with groups that use a broader form of terrorism as their calling card; groups that want the world to see how it feels to be on guard for the next drive-by shooting. *Our* groups are caught in a maze shooting at their own shadows for no apparent reason while *their* groups hit directly at the society they see as culprit. They are the advanced players in a war also birthed in powerlessness, intolerance and persecution, now turned to hate, blinding rage and revenge. Both have roots on similar ground.

While this "gang" phenomenon is an anomaly, even a perversion, their existence is part of the human condition. They are connected by response to real and imagined attacks for which they willingly give their lives in retribution, mistakenly believing that through violence they can gain power over their own lives and the lives of others. Over time their reasons to struggle have lost out to their acts of senseless brutality.

Children killing children, regardless of age or station...the thought of it is mind numbing and heart wrenching, but we prepare ourselves for the next one.

This first of three volumes explores the why and how of community violence that includes elevated levels of substance abuse, fisticuffs, family abuse, bullying and dropping out. We discuss the Rap phenomenon, the seeming allure of prison and other anti-social behaviors…and of course gangs and riots. As may surprise some, gangs are only part of the turmoil roiling particular communities. As we delve into violent neighborhoods and into the mind of the gangster we may come to better understand this upside-down world. But we also delve into the society where gangs thrive and riots happen.

This is a different picture of how and why gangs form, why youth join them and where they are headed, and a different view of relationships between society, communities, gangs and riots. The ideas and theories presented attempt to connect dots logically and offer hope for real solutions.

Some new and some classic theories are extended to the area of youth and community violence in hopes that with added knowledge new "therapies" for individuals, their communities and for societies will emerge. Youth and community violence is a solvable human and social condition but requiring cooperation among the sciences, i.e., psychology, sociology, civic and urban studies, anthropology and education and an added focus for criminology among others. You are challenged to consider a new paradigm and with it a new methodology and framework toward understanding the processes that not only induce violence but that lead to peace.

If we in America truly wish to reclaim our communities from violent youth, we must reclaim our communities from the true reasons for community violence. Then we must move boldly as if all of our own children's lives depended on it, because they do. If we are to save our communities before they slip further away, we had better begin to understand this gang violence thing.

Youth violence is community violence. And as it increases it becomes national violence. We examine this seemingly endless brutality in the microcosm that is America. And the manner and reasoning propagated for the ongoing march of youth toward violence. We discuss the child, the family, the environment and the various beliefs, theories, assumptions and even the folklore. We look at how resources are directed and some of the reasoning behind it. We also take a hard look at society and how it has operated in relation to communities engaged in violence.

As we explore these areas, tough questions will arise which the reader will be challenged to answer. It is hoped that an open discussion of these questions helps signal a new direction for the future of many of our children, including those not yet born.

Our children's future has a present that will tomorrow be a past in one form or another. I can safely say that while you ponder these written words, several people will be lost forever with youth violence as culprit. With them, a family lineage is forever vanished. And believe this, if radical changes are not made now, babies born to you today will be shooting at you tomorrow.

Our aim is to better understand how some can get to this dark place and if and how we can get them out. In so doing, we may learn lessons that go beyond this nation's borders and help achieve a more peaceful future for all of God's children.

Part 1

THE BIRTH OF A NATION DIVIDED

1

Roots to Riots

There was urgency then, there is urgency now...

> *The gang phenomenon is viewed primarily as a minority-group issue. Justice agencies struggle with how to contain them and gang researchers struggle with definitions and how to count them. And science is again attempting to follow a genetic path. Law enforcement is valiantly doing all they can to stop gangsters but to little success. No matter...for they too are fighting the wrong battle.*

Any human being is capable of violence. And violence begets violence. One must accept that violence comes in many forms.

A society can structurally help determine some aspects of behavior. People will react to positive and negative actions and the attitudes behind them. Permanent solutions to violence are not possible until symbiotic relationships between a society and her groups and communities are examined and fully understood. Similarities among groups and indeed with other cultures and societies experiencing unrest and upheaval may begin to emerge for human behavior is, after all, human behavior.

Police and gang counselors are holding tough. And they need help. To create permanent change and by that to finally cut off recruitment our sights must shift from the streets as permanent change cannot happen on the streets. To do this we must leave traditional beliefs, assumptions and hyperbole and move on to new and broader questions: Why do some persons in a social system resort to group violence as a life strategy and a way of dealing with existing conditions? Where and how did this phenomenon begin and how did it evolve? Why does it continue? What are the forces at work?

It is clear that those involved in this type of violence engage in abnormal behaviors. The most severely involved fully submerge their personal well-being for the good of the cause - *to the death.* But how did they get there individually and as a representative part of particular groups? Is there a Gestalt involved here that makes the outcome inevitable? What happened in a person's young life to turn him against what is in effect, his mirror image? And for a people, what happened in their history that turned to violent rage against each other, or even an entire society seemingly forever or to their death – whichever occurs first? And is society in any way culpable? Or is this truly a group peculiarity? Even so, in the roughest and most violent areas there are always signs of humanity.

On the face of it, part of the American gang violence process involves elimination of *enemies.* These enemies are sometimes one's own kind and sometimes others. How does this "enemies" scenario come about? Do some need to have an enemy and at the same time need to *be* an enemy? Why do some groups pass through a *gang stage* and evolve out of it, while other groups remain seemingly hopelessly entrapped, especially since the most prolific gangs seem to embrace a process of destruction whose logical end is self-elimination? What are the factors that determine if, to what degree and how long a group experiences such violence? What about those groups that once had gangs but their gangs disappeared? People seem to be imprisoning themselves. Are they responding to society's apparent disdain? Is it possible that those seemingly imprisoned do not understand any of this either? And who indeed benefits?

Is there a release process involved? Do they attack for release or is there a sociopath compulsion involved? A young person may be exhibiting identifiable and measurable sociopath behaviors even as he or she attends church, has a family and even supports community. Sadistic and masochistic behaviors may even be emerging and becoming manifest. Is this a part of the violence pattern? Are some groups genetically predisposed to violence or is there a correlation to a group's experience within a host society? When acts of varying severity occur, how is the trauma managed? Over time, does a pattern of shared violence experience result in group psychosis? Is there a state of continuing trauma affecting some groups that must be accounted for? And is society blameless in all of this? And merely left to pick up the pieces of what seems to be accepted as group sociopath behavior?

Is there also a "fear factor"? That is, as people feel more insecure or unsafe, do they feel a need to vanquish an "enemy"? Does the excitement and danger of a "gang-war" give temporary security from a fear-laden existence? Are they seeking temporary slices of "safety" perhaps as an escape from a much greater and perhaps "learned" fear such as fear of a distrustful and distrusting society? Has society effectively "cowed" some groups by lynching, raping and murdering previous generations while "obtaining" their lands, homes and businesses? In this way are they finding comfort in communal insularity, even one that includes violence mechanisms as social modifications?

There is the commonality among violent groups – *they are all minorities.* And all subjected to what seems to be *unjustified* treatment. What happens when there is no justification for ill-treatment like murder, lynching, rape and land theft? How is the seeming illogic dealt with?

Aftereffects of war and battles may also be apparent. Do they feel increasingly deadened as they engage their enemies? Do they feel even more hopeless and lost once the act is committed? Do the survivors feel guilty for their continued existence? Does "survivor guilt" or self-blame lead some to self-destruct? What part does anger play in the process? Does anger signal a retreat from solution or is it an extension of hopelessness? Is anger masking pain? Are the various self-destructive behaviors among some groups a product of externally generated shame, hopelessness, inferiority, self-deprecation and blame turned to easily aroused rage?

It is plausible that some affected persons would look to outside agents, substances and/or events to obtain (temporary) release based on their degree of fear, uneasiness and even rage. This would indicate a secondary symbiotic relationship associating substances and other self-abuse with various escapist and rage release triggers and events at varying levels and to varying degrees. Besides release, the outside agents, substances and/or events could also fulfill an unnatural and subconscious drive to self-destruct.

Could release from fear, feeling ineffectual, and the desire to self-destruct be achieved if they came to realize a real basis for their condition? What if the basis for their fearful and tortured condition is not what they have effectively internalized over generations as a negative belief structure? How effective would true knowledge be in ameliorating negative beliefs and consequent negative acts? Do the most violent areas have something more in common than gangs, drugs and violence? And if there is a relationship, can a truly comprehensive risk index be developed - a risk index that includes more than simply the individual, his peers and immediate family? For once such risk values were arrived at perhaps we would gain the ability to predict outcomes and behaviors. And from such predictive modeling ostensibly mitigate or even eliminate violent outcomes through a combination of education, treatment and structural change management, for starters. Or, we can continue as we have been and merely watch the numbers and trends and continue to count dead bodies.

The question must now be asked, "What happened or didn't happen that resulted in a group's evolving virulent community violence?" And from that, "What might be happening or not happening *now* with a particular group that may be fomenting tomorrow's violence"?

As these and many other questions and possibilities are raised, questions as to accepted explanations and solutions should also be raised. How and what are we learning that is useful and edifying from decades of strategies, analyses and ongoing battles in this multi-faceted war? Or do we simply apply political verbiage to the rising and falling numbers of the dead and injured children? As a society, we should with all that is within us delve into the very depths of what causes young people to destroy themselves and each other rather than even remotely accommodating their destruction. Instead, we have been led to stand by helplessly and view their destruction as somehow intrinsic, perhaps even genetic, that inner-city youth are somehow "hardwired" for violence even as increasing numbers of white young people join their ranks. Sure, there will always be a small percentage of persons that do bad things within any group. But the high numbers of ethnic and racial minorities involved in their own destruction begs larger questions that the easy answers we have already accepted do nothing to illuminate. Under this paradigm how can we ever find solutions?

God has made each of us for a purpose and it is not to kill and maim or waste away on drugs or in prison. He did not instill murderous hatred of ourselves and others as our pathway to Him according to group - that we picked up on our own. There is a responsibility here if we would only go there.

Some charged with researching and solving these problems look at the criminality and connect it to a people. They seek to restrict violence and criminality to their inbred behavior or genetic predisposition, and search no further. Our chronic community violence is thus divided by race and ethnicity, culture and geography, and even by victims. I offer a different view – and with it different questions.

Violence directed toward self and others may be a reaction, but to what actions? Or is it a symptom? There has to be more to it than measuring trends and counting bodies. Stop and think…many nations suffer seemingly endless cycles of violence. The reasons for their acts of brutality would seem to differentiate them. But these cycles have more in common than meets the eye. They are born of similar seeds of anger and rage. The violence occurs when rage can no longer be contained. Groups in other nations aim at the heart of their "oppressor" as American gangs turn their response inward until the top finally blows and the cycle begins anew.

Recognizing that there are cycles is not enough, for there is always a larger process in play. We must understand what sets the cycles in motion before we can know how to end them. This book helps explain that process and is intended to add to a revolution in understanding and thereby solution to the problems of youth and community violence. This book does not claim to be *thee* answer but a new way with new questions that may perhaps lead to a new understanding and a new beginning – for all of us. This book is a tool to better understand gangs and other community violence. It will challenge you to expand your thinking beyond usual explanations and theories. And as you do, other areas of impact will become evident for it is indeed past time for transformative change that has permanent impact.

This book is intended to help make peace among the children, *all of the children*. There will be no bloody scenes here. Instead, you will find reason and revelation.

There was urgency then, there is urgency now and unless we change the established patterns of all of our behaviors, the urgency will continue to move toward becoming a man-made debacle.

2

Mecca and Meltdown…

America is the home of Star-Wars and gang wars…child stars and child killing machines. Taking the form of gangland meltdown and race-war Armageddon, America is a place where growing numbers of youth are beyond angry and ready to explode. Each day thousands of community militias declare their deathly presence with bloody bursts of insurrection. And instant cold-blooded death is just a shot away.

The American dream turned nightmare for tens of thousands of our families. For with all its beauty, richness, wonders and freedom, America is a place where children murdered at the hands of other children is a major cause of death.

According to the American Academy of Pediatrics Task Force on Violence, America has the highest death rate by homicide of any of the developed nations. And teenagers more likely to die of gunshot wounds than all natural causes combined. Homicide rates for males, ages 15 to 19 increased 113 percent between 1985 and 1995, and suicide and homicide have become the second and third leading cause of death of teenagers, behind accidents, (Task Force on Violence, Jan, 1999).

FBI statistics show that incidents of youth violence bottomed in the year 2000 and began to rise up to 2004. Then in 2005 they were once again on the decline (CDC NCIPC, 2009).

This ebb and flow of teenage death is clearly a continuing national nightmare and spreading. What gives? Why in a land of so much opportunity, wealth and beauty are so many willing to terminate one another's lives? And what if any is the connection with other kinds of community violence not only here but in other lands?

...Heroes and Villains

Violence comes in many forms. Violence can be an act of physical force, meant to abuse, cause injury and death. Violence can also be covert, unseen and subtly ruinous. It can be an act of infringement, distortion and profanity. Violence can be the unjust exercising or withholding of power. Violence can occur by mischaracterizing, defining or re-defining. Whether physical or otherwise, violence can by act, treatment, behavior or procedure, traumatize those it touches. An act of violence can be a life altering experience. Violence is injurious to one degree or another.

In order for a body to heal from violence, one must know the extent of the injury, how deeply wounded and what caused the damage. Violence always has an origin, an evolution and an outcome.

How a group is received by a society can result in peace or violence to one degree or another. It is important therefore to understand the full context of origin and evolution in relation to either outcome.

Gangs...made or born?

Youth come into the world open and inquisitive. They see and feel but may not understand. A young person may well come to view the world as a place of virtue or evil and not see the shades of gray. Where there should have been a solid foundation from which to begin his journey, he finds shifting sands. And the solutions fellow travelers have found bring more confusion and danger. In some communities, violence and gangs are synonymous. But there is more to community violence than gangs.

While gangs may see themselves as a force that represents a community for all to acknowledge and fear, society sees them as criminal organizations bleeding the nation of its resources, peace and tranquility. All agree that their roots go deep. Their numbers and staying power demonstrate they fill too many young people's basic needs.

There are many reasons given for young person's joining such violent groups: peer pressure; a phase of growing up; a function of growing up in poverty; a way to success; an outlet for frustration; for protection and to defend turf from other "enemy" groups; because they're brought up that way, or as part of their culture; a manifestation of loneliness and exclusion; to gain the status and respect not obtained through legitimate means; "cause the girls dig it"; media hype. Some say it is to create a family where none exists; or a form of teen rebellion. Other reasons given include a means to express anger, fear, outrage, hate and vengeance and a way to play the chip on one's shoulder, and so on…

Joining a violent group can be to impress the girls or to play out a fantasy. It may be a statement of self-expression or even defiance; or a means of exerting emancipation and freedom; or fill a need for anger expression. There is evidence connecting group violence to poverty and social segregation (Crutchfield and Wadsworth 2003). Some hold that media violence can increase the propensity of physical and verbally aggressive behavior (Anderson et al. 2003).

On the face of it, gangs seem to be centered in the barrios, ghettos and on the reservations of America primarily among minority youth. The National Institute of Mental Health is exploring genetic links to violent behavior with research directed at inner-city youth (Stolberg 1993).

The United States Surgeon General views violence in relation to "risk factors" of the individual, family, peer and community (Office of the Surgeon General, 2001). Criminal justice agencies simply cite high crime areas and groups that reside there. But are some groups inherently violent and then form gangs to express it? Where does all of this violence come from?

Young people have their own ideas about the causes of violence, per a national survey given to youth in high-crime areas by the National Campaign to Stop Violence:

Top 10 Causes of Violence in the Order Children Cited Them:

1. The Media

2. Substance Abuse

3. Gangs

4. Unemployment

5. Weapons

6. Poverty

7. Peer Pressure

8. Broken Homes

9. Poor Family Environment / Bad Neighborhoods

10. Intolerance / Ignorance

Source: Jack Anderson. "Lucifer on the Loose" in *Meridian Magazine*, 2000. (www.meridianmagazine.com/ideas/990430looselucifer.html)

It is noteworthy that children cite media as the most influential. They seem to understand the influence of media as a primary shaper of societal behaviors (Anderson 2001).

The list cites societal issues indicating that "causes" may be being mistaken for outcomes, e. g. is media a cause of violence or do media represent a societal viewpoint? And if gangs cause violence, what causes gangs? What causes risk factors? And high-crime areas? Do currently identified causes and correlates fully account for elevated levels of community violence, or are there aspects not yet taken into account? As matters of belief and practice, gangs are considered an intransigent minority problem impossible to change except to peel off the worst actors. On that assumption, many researchers have made a career of following minority groupings around to report what they do next. Consider the following quote from one of the nation's preeminent gang researchers, Malcolm Klein:

"For the most part, gang members do very little - sleep, get up late, hang around, brag a lot, eat again, drink, hang around some more. It's a boring life; the only thing that is equally boring is being a researcher watching gang members"

—Malcolm W. Klein, 1995

Changes are reported in numbers: up or down, transitory or stable, or how they may have morphed.

So this is where we are – and have been for decades…guessing and assuming but not knowing really how or what causes gangs and violence but content to watch them as they waste away time and thus, their lives. And this is where this party begins:

3

It's a Gang Thing

Gangs and violence are synonymous. In America, gangs are big. But what is a gang? And are gangs to blame for gangs? While gangs are a significant part of today's community violence, they are only part of the violence story.

There is no set age that youth begin on the road to such violence. As far as we know, children are not predisposed with the desire to kill or be killed. But somewhere along the path, some youth cross the line from doing childhood good, to doing gangster evil. And once committed, a potent and coercive force takes control. Gangsters bask in perversions of love, happiness and well-being, thriving in a world built on aberrations of power, glory and respect, killing and dying over these as though they were renowned badges of honor. Though there are different kinds of violent youth and the groups they belong to the outcome is the same: the elimination of young people and the slow internal death of the remaining combatants. As children consider the gang lifestyle, there is little thought given to the invisible chains of slavery implicit in the gang contract and its accompanying grief. The gangster road is tough and one that a person would not seem to willingly choose. So why do so many children get to this place? Is it by nature? Is it by nurture? And just how many youth are involved? And to what degree? Where do they all come from? But always, why?

Gang models, patterns and confusion:

There are varieties of gangs. However, most attention is directed at the so-called *Traditional* gang: the urban, minority gang. In this classic gang paradigm, youthful gangsters keep it simple: they murder their own kind.

In the broader gang paradigm, youth from all walks engage in deadly violence adding to the plethora of labels as it progresses: school shootings, freeway shootings, race-related, drug-related, turf-related, gang-related, rage-related or simply random acts of violence. But it is all children eliminating other children. Confusion reigns over this destructive part of our society. Defining and tabulating who makes up violent youth, the groups they belong to and the number of youth on this path is highly subjective and at best, imprecise.

Descriptions and methods of tabulation can be confusing. In 1997, the Office of Juvenile Justice and Prevention's James C. Howell, Ph. D., observed that, *"There is no single, accepted definition. State and local jurisdictions tend to develop their own. Nevertheless, a youth gang is commonly thought of as a self-formed association of peers having the following characteristics: a gang name and recognizable symbols, identifiable leadership, a geographic territory, a regular meeting pattern, and collective actions to carry out illegal activities"* (Howell, 1997).

Finn-Aage Esbennsen points out the fundamental problem in this area stating: *"As a general observation, gang research in the United States suffers from definitional shortcomings and calls into question its ability to inform policy makers and expand criminological knowledge. There is little, if any, consensus as to what constitutes a gang and who is a gang member, let alone what gangs do, either inside or outside the law..."* (Esbensen, Winfree, He, & Taylor, 2001).

The Department of Justice's National Gang Center (NGC), (formerly National Youth Gang Center, NYGC) annual survey of law enforcement agencies allows flexibility in this area as reporting agencies made it clear they use a wide variety of characteristics to define youth gangs. Since 1996, the NGC has used the following definition: *"a group of youths or young adults in your jurisdiction that you or other responsible persons in your agency or community are willing to classify as a 'gang.'"* Here, the NGC is allowing the broadest of definitions without guidelines.

In order of priority, the top six law enforcement criteria are:

➢   *commits crimes together;*

➢   *has a name;*

➢   *hangs out together;*

➢   *claims a turf or territory of some sort;*

➢   *displays/wears common colors or other insignia, and;*

➢   *has a leader(s)* (Howell, James C & Arlen Egley, Jr., 2010).

There is need for caution in endorsing such a protocol.

Leaving the classification of a gang and gang member to "responsible persons in your agency or community" invites bias. Even with the best intentions measures may be adopted that may conflict with civil rights that can cause irreparable damage to lives and futures. Many cities have adopted a "zero-tolerance" to anything that appears gang related which is open to interpretation and possible over-reaction.

In Bonita Springs, Florida a 22 year-old Latino college student with a photo of himself wearing a baseball cap and mimicking a gang member sent via the Internet was arrested with several others for *"electronically promoting gangs"* over the Internet, a third degree felony (Naples News, 2008).

Cities are adopting gang registries using various determinants. Santa Fe, New Mexico outlawed the Virgin Mary on clothing. Many cities are considering banning baggy pants, now a fashion mode featured in clothing advertising and sold in most clothing stores. This "fashion" began originally in poor families for children to wear hand me downs, and clothes large enough to last through growth spurts. Belts were a luxury (NPR 2007).

The RICO statutes (Racketeer Influenced and Corrupt Organizations Act) originally intended for use against the Mafia is at times being applied to impetuous minority youth playing out a modern version of James Dean-like rebellion or fantasy "dress-up" and collecting felony records in the process as seen with the young man in Florida. These desperate actions occur when true understanding of what causes gangs and violence remain unknown.

In contrast to over-reaction is under-reaction. Several cases of hate gang activity have occurred in recent years where the gang element was ignored as well as other criminal aspects of the events. To wit: *"Prosecutors called the beating death of an illegal immigrant from Mexico a hate crime, and they urged an all-white jury in Pennsylvania coal country to punish two white teenagers for their roles in the attack. Instead, the jury found the teens innocent of all serious charges, a decision that elicited cheers and claps from the defendants' families and friends — and cries of outrage from the victim's,"* (The Associated Press, 2009).

And one reported by Chicago Tribune correspondent Howard Witt Tribune on June 5, 2005 from Linden, Texas: *"They picked up Billy Ray Johnson outside a convenience store in this East Texas bayou town, a place where Confederate flags fly in some front yards and a mural of barefoot slaves picking cotton greets patrons inside the local post office. On a cool September night in 2003, they drove the 42-year-old mentally retarded black man to a cow pasture where a crowd of white youths was having a party. They got Johnson drunk, they made him dance, they jeered at him with racial epithets. Then, according to court testimony, one of Johnson's assailants punched him in the face, knocking him out cold. They tossed his unconscious body into the back of a pickup and dumped him by the side of a dirt road, on top of a mound of stinging fire ants. Johnson, who family members say functioned at the level of a 12-year-old before the attack, was in a coma for a week. He suffered a brain hemorrhage that slurred his speech, weakened his legs and deprived him of his ability to take care of himself. His body was covered with hundreds of painful ant bites. Today he lives on public assistance, confined to a nursing home in nearby Texarkana, where his family fears he will have to remain for the rest of his life (Witt 2005)."* Four young white men convicted in the case were given light sentences with three receiving 30 days and a fourth 60 days in jail. The Southern Poverty Law Center took the case to civil court and won a $9 million verdict on Billy Ray's behalf (Southern Poverty Law Center 2007).

These and many others like them are hard-core crimes committed by gangs of youth. They fit a category of terrorism as they are aimed at a people with the intent and effect of creating generalized terror among that population but are ignored as such. Such bias encourages additional violence against targeted groups, all of which generates rage and the potential for reactionary violence.

Tracking and research...

Law enforcement generally relies on gang researchers for guidance. Most research is after the fact and follows changes in numbers and appearance and offers explanation. Malcolm Klein, noted career gang researcher of over thirty-five years, unveiled a six-tier model that classifies gangs across the nation by number and longevity (Klein & Maxson, 1996). This information illustrates how serious our gang problem has become over time. But which gangs are included and excluded? And why did they form? What brought them into being? According to Klein, Howell, Egley, Spergel, Gleason and other noted gang researchers, gang members have been primarily young adult males from homogeneous lower class, inner-city, ghetto or barrio neighborhoods (Klein, 1995; Miller, 1992; Moore, 1990, 1991; Spergel, 1995) that are racially/ethnically segregated. They have been actively involved in a variety of criminal activities, including drug trafficking (Howell, Egley, Gleason, OJJDP Bulletin June, 2002). Research, definitions and thus perceptions agree that street gangs are distinctive to minority populations. Gang research tracks activity and little beyond that.

Gang research appears to acquiesce to monitoring and arrests of youthful minority male groupings that "responsible persons" determine is a gang. This profile could logically include a group of minority youngsters hanging out in a park, at a theater, on a street corner or in front of a private residence, and oftentimes does with tragic results.

In barrios, ghettos and on reservations, the terms, *youth gang* and *street gang* are used interchangeably. Law enforcement keep a close eye and collect data on potential members and emerging gangs in these locales relying on visual observation of dress and colors. For the most part, research defines non-ethnic white violence as *transitory* (without longevity) so avoid such attention, e.g., the Columbine bunch would not be classified as a violent youth gang - new, emerging or otherwise. By contrast, a similarly outfitted grouping of African-American, Native American, Asian and Latino youth may likely be considered suspect and often-times is. Such is a weakness with current methods. Current practice separates groups along racial and ethnic lines in perception, belief, theory and practice. It would be more appropriate to view gangs and violence as a fundamental intra-societal structural problem that can trigger group violence.

From the Office of Juvenile Justice and Delinquency Prevention Juvenile Justice Bulletin, June 2002, <u>Modern-Day Youth Gangs,</u> discussing the increase of non-ethnic white youth gangs in small cities and in rural areas: *"The spread of gangs beyond central cities in the 1980s and 1990s (Miller, 2001; NYGC, 1999a, 1999b, 2000) raises the question of whether the newer gangs forming in cities, small towns, and suburban and rural areas are different from the traditional inner-city gangs, as has been suggested by Curry (1999); Howell and Gleason (1999), Howell, Moore and Egley (2001); and Starbuck, Howell, and Lindquist (2001)"*. The bulletin concludes that *"Gangs in the late-onset jurisdictions had younger members, slightly more females, and more of a racial/ethnic mixture; were less involved in drug trafficking; and were less involved in violent crimes, including homicides."* The report continues: *"Although Caucasians were the predominant racial/ethnic group in (these) later onset (1991 or later) localities, racial/ethnic mixing may be a defining characteristic of such gangs"*.

This research concludes that although there are gangs and white youth are the predominant members, racial/ethnic mixing *"may be a defining characteristic"*. This could be interpreted as assigning responsibility for the emergence and spread of youth gangs to "racial/ethnic mixing". This may also be interpreted as a subtle argument *to maintain separation of groups*. It misses an opportunity to suggest investigation into fundamental processes that result in all gang emergence.

The report states that gender mixing was also common (Esbensen and colleagues 1999), *"92 percent of eighth grade gang members said that both boys and girls belonged to their gangs"*. The actions of the youth were tracked to determine if they were *"different from the traditional inner-city gangs"*. Again, we are directed to the perceived nucleus of gangs: *inner-city minority youth*. Such assumptions may be reason that systemic solutions are not considered. The larger questions of *why* there are violent youth groups/gangs anywhere remains unasked and therefore unexplored, except to return to the minority, inner-city paradigm.

The fundamental underpinnings and origins of "gangs" remain unexamined. We *do* know enough to ask if they are spreading and race/ethnic and gender mixing. Upon further reading, the reports tend to support a contention of relief, if you will that **these** groups are **not** as dangerous as where the minority youth presumably came from. The issue of race/ethnic mixing would seem to be raised as a cautionary note for parents as re: who their children pick as friends while explaining hybrid-like gang-trending observed in some communities. Perhaps current beliefs about this "gangster mystique" are why some confusion persists. Like society, the universe of youth violence is ever changing. It is not simply single race, colors and turf related killings. Youth violence can be as diverse as a society and dynamics within it. "The gangster mystique is attracting young people from all walks" (Howell, Egley and Gleason, 2002).

To gather a more complete youth violence picture, the current practice of limiting (and directing) gang definitions, questions, numbers, perceptions and research by race/ethnicity, location and longevity should be abandoned in favor of a broader, inclusive investigation.

Today's youth violence is not a modern version of the Hatfields and McCoys or *West Side Story*. Contemporary gangs range from mild to wild.

Some are here today and gone tomorrow. But many are more brutal and have phenomenal growth and staying power.

For many young people who end up at Gangdom's door, it is the wholesale acceptance of dying hopes and dreams, pasts and futures, with no stake in any of it. Believing they have only "the moment" to live for, they are maxing it out. They have reached the point of giving up on their futures and themselves, burying budding spirits in alcohol, drugs and nasty habits. For others, it is a way to express collective outrage.

For America's minority youth, belonging to a violent group is convenient and even expected. They serve in their neighborhood militias, ready to defend their opaque homeland against their latest deadly enemies - going on daily search and destroy missions in winless battles against their own images. These children are driven to kill and be killed in their simple but bloody orgy of socially defiant behavior. They have found a greater cause to live and die for than their own worthless selves. These youth are ready and willing to die a quicker death than the walking ghosts around them. To this end they believe they have found a just cause – one in which they can shine as bright as a falling star and go down in a blaze of glory.

For gang groupies and wannabes, it is carrying the gangster fantasy dangerously far. Their rebellion and anti-hero worship can turn deadly with a flash of gunfire, making them the latest lemming to be in the wrong place at the wrong time. They push their luck with clothing, attitude and associations. They are toying on deadly ground, coming perilously close to submerging their identities, values and dreams to become part of this extended but violent family. For all new entrants into the world of gang violence, the door is there as it has always been, left ajar for the curious, the wandering and the lost. They venture in but may never make it back from this cold and deadly managed care program intended for the unwanted.

This is serious stuff. Whether we label it youth rebellion, another lost generation, urban terrorism or simply a gang state-of-mind matters little to those who believe in their souls that they have nothing else to live for. The perception that one must belong to a street gang is no longer a prerequisite to youth violence. Incidents of peer murder among seemingly disassociated young people are more common. Some are even acting as if they were in a gang of one. It is the *why* of such violence we must examine in all its varied aspects and possibilities.

In the meantime, something has changed. Many of the *traditional* players in this deadly game are not behaving as predictably as before. Many have come to believe that their community's gang violence is a result of a nasty game being played on them and are laying down their arms and ending their anger release against their own people. Where rage previously could be counted on to be inward directed, there is transition in belief and action, some positive and some not. And white youth *are* involved. They may act from a different circumstance *but they are reacting similarly.*

As devastating as it is, forming or belonging to any violent group is probably the least understood activity that youth engage in. They share common ground. Others have gone before them. Their rage is not new. They are all human and they react within understandable human parameters. It is not as mysterious or as hopeless as it would seem. But we have to move beyond stereotypes, erroneous and biased assumptions and antiquated research methods.

4

Who's on First?

The method of keeping track of violent youth reminds one of the pre-9/11 chaos where numerous governmental agencies were responsible for our national security but were not in the same book let alone the same page. There are plenty of people hired, but the work product does not reflect progress. As the 9/11 Commission indicated, the problem was not that information was not available or that not enough people were employed, we just did not understand the dynamics of what we were looking at (Kean et al. 2004).

In America, violent youth gangs were *recognized* during the 19th Century (English, 1991; Ungar, 1995; Fried, 1993; Repetto, 2004). Then they were mainly Irish, Polish, Jewish and Italian. Others evolved or arrived during the 20th Century, but we did not keep official government tabs on them until a few years ago as the expansion and seeming intractability of our latest gangs had given the matter significance. As earlier noted, the National Gang Center (NGC) under the Department of Justice is the national repository for gang information. According to the NGC, the first ever national gang survey was completed in 1982. It compared 1967 to 1980 but counted known major gang cities only (Miller, 2001).

That survey indicated that in 1967, gangs numbered in the low one-hundreds, and there were 181 gang deaths. In 1980 there were 2,000 gangs in 286 jurisdictions representing 100,000 gang members, and gang deaths numbered 633.

More than fifteen years later, NGC released the results of *their* first survey conducted in 1995. The respondents were a sampling of law enforcement agencies from around the country. That year's data revealed phenomenal growth: 24,000 gangs in 2,000 cities including Alaska and Hawaii with membership of 664,000. Their 1996 report showed an increase to 31,000 gangs in 4,824 jurisdictions with membership exceeding 846,000. These numbers did not include white gangs, motorcycle gangs, militia, anarchists, Satanists, skinheads or neo-Nazis. Mafia-like groups in Chicago and Los Angeles were not included nor were prison gangs or Native Americans. Those tallied under this heading were *traditional* inner-city minority gangs with particular clothing, hairstyles and tattoos and identifiable territories with some history (National Youth Gang Center; released 1999).

However, the following year's report (1996) indicated the face of gangs was changing. From the 1996 survey (released 1999), *"The race and ethnicity of gang members appear to be changing compared with earlier national surveys."* The report stated that *"the proportions of Caucasian/white gang members in rural counties (32%) and small cities (31%) was more than twice the national average and was now the fastest-growing segment of violent youth groups"*. Respondents in the 1996 survey reported the following *overall* gang numbers: Hispanic/Latino: 44%; African-American: 35%; Caucasian/White: 14%; Asian: 5%; other: 2%. The report also stated, *"...in self-reporting surveys, students often report much higher numbers, especially Caucasian/white"*.

Increasingly draconian measures were being adopted in many jurisdictions that would place gang members behind bars for longer durations, topped by "three strikes and life" in prison. As earlier stated, since Columbine and similar incidents, and as reports of increasing white youth involvement (hybrid gangs) came in, the depth of research expanded to conclude that Caucasian/white participation would be considered "transitory", that they leave the local violent group behind when they graduate high school and move on to their futures (Howell and Egley 2005).

The reporting of white youth participation took an abrupt turn. According to 2001 law enforcement respondents, *"nearly half (49 percent) of all gang members were Hispanic/Latino, 34 percent African American/black, 10 percent Caucasian/white, 6 percent Asian, and the remainder of another race/ethnicity"* (Egley Jr and Ritz 2006). *"A decreasing trend in white youth involvement is noted while all others are increasing"* (Howell and Egley 2005). However, as earlier noted, changing demographics were still reason for concern. From the bulletin: *"The fastest-growing ethnic group in the United States is Latinos. This ethnic group has grown to be the second-largest group in the country, to approximately 40 million in 2003 (The Tomás Rivera Policy Institute, 2004). Latinos are now the largest ethnic minority in nearly half of the states, and their numbers are growing fastest in the South, although the largest Latino concentrations are in the West, South Florida, and a few large cities."* The report again downplays white youth gang-like misbehavior explaining the *"emergence or escalation of gang problems"* is due to *"changing demographics"*. By 2010, according to the National Gang Center FAQ, Caucasian white would now now officially make up only 7% of gangs (Howell and Egley, Jr 2010). The change in how Caucasian white youth gang involvement is viewed and therefore counted remains.

A clue to gang behavior

Nonetheless, Columbine was one of a series of earthquakes to youth violence research. The trend to violence by white youth was unforeseen, embarrassing and very disturbing. Simplistic answers would not suffice here. Research was re-tooled to get to the bottom of it, and had been starting to. According to the National Gang Center (FAQ, Pt.2), one gang researcher had outlined four community conditions that often precede the transition from typical adolescent groupings to established youth gangs (Moore, 1998).

➤ The first is that families and schools are ineffective and alienating and conventional adult supervision is for the most part, absent;

➤ Secondly, adolescents have a great deal of free time that is consumed by unhealthy social development roles;

➤ Third, gangs take hold when youth have limited access to appealing conventional career lines;

➤ and finally, young people must have a place to gather.

These four conditions generally fit the profile of an inner-city minority community: a *"disorganized community"*.

As earlier noted gang research attributes much of white youth gang involvement to "racial and ethnic mixing" and MTV and is "transitory" at worst. There had been growing numbers of white participation and still is. But structural social supports were in place to receive these prodigal young people as they grew out of it. Indeed, the four conditions where gangs emerge seem to confirm this view by identifying *fundamental differences* between communities where gangs become permanent and thrive *(disorganized communities)* and where they do not, thus allaying fears of gang permanence among white youth.

Our experience at CYGS confirms Moore's observations, especially as relates to the "schools are ineffective" and "appealing career lines" aspects. Quality education and resources are how a society advances. A double standard has evolved over the history of this nation: one that promotes social advancement and one that does not. We need to delve deeper into systemic designs to get to source and evolution and connect these to **outcomes,** as *the larger elements that result in either relative peace or violence among youth are structural.*

The United States Secret Service also looked into the matter. Their investigation and conclusions dealt with Columbine and other school shootings. Although not stated as such, their findings illustrate commonality between white killers and minority gangsters in that they both *have grievances, access to weapons* and are *depressed or despondent* (Secret Service study Oct., 2000). These three aspects appear to be consistent with the conditions pointed out by Moore.

Programs immediately sprang up to deal with middle-class youth angst. Their structural supports were fine. However, this discussion brings into focus where society might invest resources *if* society were serious about ending the bloody carnage in disorganized (minority) communities. Youth see the differences in schools, libraries, parks and playgrounds; even differences in streets and sewers. And they know where financial resources are going for "solutions" rather than to make fundamental structural changes that would permanently improve outcomes.

We have seen periodic inner-city experiments involving improved educational materials and equipment. Teachers were uplifted and students rose to the occasion. These efforts are rare exceptions and not the rule. And then there are stories of inner-city heroics by an individual teacher or school principal raising the hopes and spirits of children while in their presence. This is *not* structural improvement. What these do prove is that these young people are eager to learn and ready to take on challenges if and when given the tools and opportunity to do so. The talent is there on both sides waiting through generations to be tapped.

Instead, "solutions" are geared to the unfortunate outcomes of such a scheme. These are led by law enforcement and the prison industrial complex and the hundreds of millions of dollars invested through them. This institutional complex has experienced massive growth (US Bureau of Justice Statistics 2010). The reliance on enforcement and imprisonment has nothing to do with structural underpinnings of community disorganization and subsequent community violence. Alas, these agencies were placed in this untenable position and are simply doing their best to keep the violence down.

The FBI oversees national anti-gang efforts, including data gathering and analysis. In a 1997 statement before the US Senate, Steven R. Wiley, the chief of the FBI's Violent Crimes and Major Offenders Section stated the following: *"Two of the basic obstacles in addressing gang activity in communities around the nation is the absence of a universal definition for gangs, and the difficulty in documenting the nature and extent of gang related criminal activity. While some communities acknowledged difficulties in dealing with the problem, they failed to concede that they have a gang problem until the gangs become firmly entrenched".* The FBI chief then gave the official overview for contemporary street gang violence: *"While street gangs may specialize in entrepreneurial activities like drug dealing, their gang related lethal violence is more likely to grow out of turf conflicts than from the entrepreneurial activity. Drug markets indirectly influenced violence by bringing rival gang members into proximity with one another, as most street gang violence involves inter-gang conflicts".* He continued, *"By far the most visible and frightening of gang crimes is murder. Contrary to popular belief, most murders committed by gang members are not random shootings nor are they direct disputes over drugs or some other crime. While these types of gang homicides do occur, most are the products of old-fashioned fights over* **turf, status and revenge**. *Drive-by shootings and other confrontations of this kind typically involve small sets of gang members acting more or less on their own, not large groups representing the entire gang. But each attack creates a chain reaction of complicity, vengeance and commitment (Wiley, S, 1997)."* The FBI Chief pointed out a few major points that guide the thoughts about street gangs:

➢ the reluctance or outright failure of communities to recognize local gang problems until they were firmly entrenched;

➢ that gangs are composed of ethnic persons that mainly kill each other over *turf, status and revenge;* and

➢ that once a group becomes involved, an ongoing chain reaction is put into place that commits the gang to further violence.

The latter two points describes the so-called gang *cycle of violence* that underpins modern gang understanding.

Researchers are identifying mixed or hybrid groups as noted earlier. However, the *turf, status and revenge* rationale has been and continues to be the litmus test for mainline, or what are commonly referred to as *Traditional gangs*: minority youth in disorganized communities. Some dismiss hybrid groupings as a phase of growing up. However, a closer look at Hybrid Gangs as part of a social evolutionary process reveals useful information.

From the Institute for Governmental Research: *"Question: Are today's youth gangs different from gangs in the past? Answer: Some of the gangs that have emerged in the past decade are noticeably different from those that emerged before the mid-1980's (Howell, Egley, and Gleason, 2002; Howell, Moore, and Egley, 2002). These gangs are commonly described as having a "hybrid gang culture", meaning they do not follow the same rules or methods of operation, making documentation and categorization difficult, they may have several of the following characteristics: a mixture of racial/ethnic groups; a mixture of symbols and graffiti associated with different gangs; wearing colors traditionally associated with a rival gang; less concern over turf or territory; and members who sometimes switch from one gang to another.Members of contemporary gangs often 'cut and paste' bits of Hollywood images and big-city gang lore into their local versions of gangs (Starbuck, Howell, and Lindquist, 2001)".*

So-called Hybrid gangs have in their number youth wanting to engage in illegal economic activities. They also attract young people who are more rebellious than committed to dying over graffiti or turf, including groupies and trend followers. Hybrid groupings are also a haven for disaffected youth of a new generation, some of whom may eventuate to committing violence.

But all of this was also true during evolutionary stages of Traditional gangs.

There is *always* a beginning. Chronic elevated levels of community violence does not just happen, it evolves. The emergence of Hybrids should again wake up researchers who remain stuck on a racial and ethnic track and dismiss early warning signs of white youth's participation in violence and other antisocial behaviors.

➢ Hybrids are an indicator of growing acceptance of the gang culture as a vehicle for an increasing number of disaffected youth.

➢ Hybrids indicate negatively evolving critical mass where large numbers are changed mentally and emotionally.

➢ Hybrid gangs belie previously accepted definitions that gangs can be identified by turf, uniform or colors or even race and ethnicity.

Race-mixing is not the culprit, any more than African-Americans or Latino Americans are responsible for evolving Crips and barrio homeboys. This should be placed in the context of social evolution.

In a fast moving and changing youth violence environment, various researchers including the former NYGC (now NGC) of the Justice Department are attempting to keep track of and explain groups of youthful killers. Following trends and counting numbers while surreptitiously finding reasons to exclude white youth do not help explain *why* youth in any community engage in violence. One violent child is one too many. Eight hundred thousand or so (ethnic gang count only) is a societal nightmare that requires a concentrated and studied look that ignores politics of race or ethnicity.

The 1996 NYGC report stated, and affirmed by the FBI chief, that for various reasons some jurisdictions do not want to classify violent youth activity as such or refuse to track them at all (Office of Juvenile Justice and Delinquency Prevention 1999). And some jurisdictions state that their youth groups only participate in "gang-like" behavior. Many cities and towns want to place blame for their violent youth anywhere but home.

Popularly, Los Angeles and South of the border are the places most blamed for the explosion of gang problems: that they physically exported their reign of terror to unsuspecting cities small and large all over the USA. And between the Bloods and Crips and South of the border gangsters, gangs were out of local control, but through no fault of the locals. But a 1992 gang migration study of 1,100 targeted cities found that *"most cities had local gangs before the onset of migration, and many respondents felt that their city would have a gang problem regardless of migration"* (Maxson et al., 1996, p. 29). There has been what amounts to a collective resistance to admitting that violent youth are growing in our own backyards, in our own soils and from our own seed.

In addition, confusion in classifying violent youth activity remains as to what constitutes gang related vs. gang motivated criminal activity (Langston, 2003). For example, in Los Angeles and other cities, if gang members kill someone while hijacking their car, raping a family member or robbing a home, or a child is killed while playing on the sidewalk or while sleeping in his bed in a botched gang drive-by shooting it is not considered "gang related" as the victim did not belong to a gang. If a gang member kills another gang member over a drug deal gone bad or over sales territory, it is not a gang murder but is instead "drug related".

However, if the perpetrator(s) *and* victim(s) are both members of gangs and the motive for a murder can be proven to be over *turf, status or revenge,* then is it counted as a gang murder regardless of other factors. E.g. a gang member is killed on home turf in a drive-by shooting *(turf)*; a gang member disrespects another gang member by word or deed and is killed for the act *(status)*; a payback killing over an earlier gang-related murder *(revenge).* This paradigm applies to **Traditional** minority gangs only and does not apply to violent activities other groups engage in. This downplays and confuses the violence issue and is counterproductive to finding solutions and does not assist society in ameliorating the youth violence phenomenon.

Attempts to classify and define "gangs" may be honest efforts to understand and deal more effectively with the groups involved in criminality. However, a de-facto separation along racial and ethnic lines is dangerous for all. When the Columbine incident occurred, all manner of research, analysis, discovery and solutions were directed at the malady presented.

All youth violence should be considered with resources directed at structural reasons for the deadly outcomes without regard to race and ethnicity. We cannot get to the bottom line issues if we are content to allocate the problem according to group and outward appearances, which are changeable.

The NGC is the first government agency to attempt to gather information, qualify and quantify the gang violence phenomenon in America. They accumulate and disseminate research and report what law enforcement officers observe in various parts of the country. As noted earlier, such reporting is subject to interpretation. In addition, they are trailing indicators, in some cases delayed from two to five years. This is not a pure science. But still the question must be asked, "Is this the best we can do?"

As indicated by the FBI spokesman, tallying gang statistics can be difficult and imprecise. The National Gang Center began collecting and analyzing data in 1985. As of 2008 and multi-millions of dollars later, unsettling problems remain with analysis and data gathering with respect to violent groups including basic definition, crime attribution and inclusion. Defining and tallying numbers already trails reality by years and counts some and ignores others. Such are the consequences of following *outcomes*. By definition, *outcomes* do not provide clues to origins or process.

All indications are that this nation continues to experience a sustained gang membership drive. It is the author's educated opinion that if *all* violent groups were counted, the one-millionth gangster is already born and preparing for their role in society. There are untold numbers engaged in drive-bys, drug murders, carjacking, home invasions, race-murders, robberies, rapes, school shootings, park shootings and whatever new mayhem and terminology comes into vogue, and of course over *turf, status* and *revenge.* Who does what and how the numbers and appearances change is important but not as important as understanding why they exist at all. Do we continue to accept and promote that minority youth are somehow intrinsically, even genetically prone to violence and continue to profile, count, analyze and intercept them at ever younger ages and dismiss the rest? Or do we dig deep and ask why is it that this death process even exists?

There is no way to be sure of actual numbers of all youth lost to overall violent gang/group activity (NYGC, 1999b). According to the FBI Uniform Crime Report, updated 02/17/2006, total numbers of gang homicides from 2000 to the end of 2004 were 718; 958; 986; 933 and 899 respectively (anyone knowledgeable about gangs will attest these are serious undercounts). These numbers account for approximately seven percent of total homicides for each year during the period. At this annual rate of 900 gang deaths per year, by the end of the first quarter of the new millennium, as many as 22,500 youth will have died at the hands of other children. There are 22,500 more good reasons to get to the bottom of why gangs exist and thrive.

Over my twenty-five year career, I have found that gangs and the youth that comprise them are not dissimilar in various parts of the country. In fact, they are very much the same regardless of group or location. What *is* highly variable is the degree of knowledge and belief about an area's violent youth, especially how and why they came into being. Many simply accept that such violence is endemic to minority groups. Tracking, isolation, containment and force remain the solutions.

...a simple fact

Turf, status and revenge have stood as the official reasons for gang violence. Acts of youth violence are screened via this tri-causal interpretation applying to ethnic and racial minority persons. This is actually a false screen.

In point of fact, not one gang member ever killed another person with turf, status or revenge as cause. These are "triggers" to violent actions and have nothing to do with what causes them.

These triggers are end-stage results of very real fundamental reasons for violence and for the development of gangs in the first place. The *turf, status and revenge* rationale is at best a tragic grand oversimplification

with serious implications including that it impedes knowledge and thereby delays and even subverts permanent, structural solution.

Successful intervention relies on full understanding of origins and evolutionary processes to understand violent outcomes. Then we may target each stage and phase effectively and efficiently. Reacting to events is not only inaccurate, it is not proactive nor is it cost-effective. It is obvious that 'triggering events' are being confused with causes. The biggest surprise of all may be that the youth involved in such violence do not understand the issue of youth violence either. When "triggered" they simply fire away! They also need answers to the same timeless questions. They do not delve beneath the obvious blood and guts level to see the context of their group's existence in a social schematic or their part in it.

Despite appearances to the contrary, I have witnessed that many hardened gang members are not comfortable in their high-risk lifestyle. They do not understand why they are in a violent group or why they do what they do. Nor do they understand why they are willing in many cases, to lay down their lives supposedly over *turf, status or revenge.* As they themselves will tell you, "That's just the way it is, man". If and when he finally figures it out, it is usually too late.

They will contribute...they will produce... they will advance... and they will succeed... *at something*.... even failure. They will not disappear nor will their groups go away. It is my honest and firm belief that most persons even from the most crime-ridden communities would rather be productive, functioning and upwardly mobile members of society, including those who eventually become gang members.

In moments of honesty, a hardened gangster will often acknowledge that he does not like the gangster life. His involvement seems almost involuntary.

The most telling evidence of this is that he will do almost anything to keep his younger relatives from following in his footsteps. He cites feelings of being trapped, or being in too far to get out or that it's too late for him and his life is over even though he may only be in his 20s. But he will beg from a tattered heart to please, *please* concentrate on his siblings and/or his children to keep them out.

This negative response to his practiced behavior belies what he has accepted as his place in life. Yet he continues to play the hand dealt as if programmed to do so, behaving as if he is a hopeless case. No one has told him any different...on the contrary. His group is socially structured to be separate from one world and part of another. He follows what he believes to be his path in life. However, his beliefs and his behavior are deviant substitutes in an aberrant environment. Much of what he has learned from both worlds must and can be undone.

Euphemisms such as "school violence" are coined for the spread of youth violence beyond traditional arenas in an effort to separate away and contain what is actuality a new strain of an old disease. Schools, our children's learning centers, have long been scenes of violence in so-called "disorganized communities". As non-traditional areas become affected, schools increasingly spend limited funds to transform into makeshift prisons. We continue to engage in classic overreactions to events, rather than working to understand and ameliorate the fundamental causes of youth violence.

As we attack the perception, the reality has escaped and moved on. The youth are not where we thought they were or are targeting. We are shocked and surprised at the new directions that youth are going and wonder why we always seem to be behind the youth violence curve trying desperately to catch up. We wonder why we just cannot seem to stop the inflow of youngsters into this death-defying lifestyle. In spite of multi-layered fixes, tougher sentences, tighter monitoring and expensive jail time, we appear impotent. Most researchers, practitioners as well as the youth involved have not a clue as to the real reasons youth are eliminating each other. Yet this is the basic question *not* being addressed at its core.

5

Universal Pain in the Gang Universe

America has endured many plights, plagues and troubles. When faced with such, we move quickly to eradicate them at the source. The Center for Disease Control and Prevention (CDCP) and the Surgeon General of the United States have proclaimed youth violence to be a public health issue affecting the lives and well being of millions of American families (CDCP, Factsheet, 2005; DHHS 2001) This marks the first time agencies of the US government made a connection between youth violence and public health. The National Institute of Mental Health (NIMH9) has also entered this arena but in a way that should raise some concerns...

With respect to America's longstanding youth violence problem, the justice system led the response. "Gang leaders" and "gang infrastructure" were some of the first targets, as though a monolithic gang brain-trust were breeding super-gangsters who led legions of havoc-producing minions forth against society. But as fast as we locked them up or they died, younger replacements competed for position.

The solutions were then directed at the home, so parent classes and parental punishments were tried. Still the violence continued. Then were the roundups, photo indexing of children, and then the domains...

The CDCP and NIMH are pointing at research, prevention and treatment. The justice system must remain focused on perpetrators.

However, some of the NIMH research involves "genetic predispositions" to violence. This raises concern due to statements on the NIMH website:

"Tragic events like the shootings at Columbine High School capture public attention and concern, but are not typical of youth violence. Most adolescent homicides are committed in inner-cities outside of school. They most frequently involve an interpersonal dispute and a single victim. On average, six or seven youths are murdered in this country each day. Most of these are inner-city minority youths. Such acts of violence are tragic and contribute to a climate of fear in schools and communities." And further down the page, *"...research on differences in the magnitude of genetic and environmental influences on different kinds of conduct problems is providing a key to understanding the developmental origins of antisocial behavior. Many twin and adoption studies indicate that child and adolescent antisocial behavior is influenced by both genetic and environmental factors, suggesting that genetic factors directly influence cognitive and temperamental predispositions to antisocial behavior. These predisposing child factors and socializing environments, in turn, influence antisocial behavior. Research suggests that for some youth with early onset behavior problems, genetic factors strongly influence temperamental predisposition, particularly oppositional temperament, which can affect experiences negatively. When antisocial behavior emerges later in childhood or adolescence, it is suspected that genetic factors contribute less, and such youths tend to engage in delinquent behavior primarily because of peer influences and lapses in parenting. The nature of the child's social environment regulates the degree to which heritable early predisposition results in later antisocial behavior."* www.nimh.nih.gov/ **02**/2006).

Science may be following a pre-conceived notion. Human beings *are* capable of violence in given situations. Violence is a human defense mechanism as well as tool to secure continued existence through natural and manmade turmoil. Since gangs do not have enemies of nature, it would seem more productive to investigate the *manmade turmoil* inasmuch as the NGC, FBI and gang researchers attribute gang violence and its' spread to the "inner city" and its inhabitants.

eugenics is never far away…

The National Institute of Mental Health (NIMH) now accepts *"heritable predisposing violence influences"* that can be connected to biological common denominators that relate to a group(s), and that such violence occurs mostly with *"inner-city minority youth"*. As a support, the "discovery" of a so-called "warrior gene" is asserted by Florida State's Kevin Beaver, to wit: *"Beaver's study shows a direct link between boys who have the specific variant of the MAOA gene, called the 'low-activity 3-repeat allele,' to gang membership and participation in gun violence. What this means, is that scientists finding the warrior gene in boys can predict gang membership, based on the existence of the gene variant alone".* (www.physorg.com/news163419590.html**)**

This is *really* scary stuff.

If this logic is to be followed then it is appropriate for the original Colonists and the heroes of the Boston Tea Party be included in these studies as they were seen by many as angry militants, violent anarchists, traitors, terrorists and murderers who rioted and fought their legal government. These community reactionaries perceived their English governors as oppressors. Were those who engaged in this behavior genetically predisposed to violence?

Irish, Italians, Poles, Jews, and other immigrant groups experienced similar negative experiences when relocating here albeit not as severe as Native Americans, African-Americans, Asians and Latinos and formed gangs but their gangs disappeared. All of these groups except Italians and Asians formed gangs after arriving here. Italians and Asians had similar social experiences in their native countries. They too must be included in these DNA studies.

And of Civil War patriots on both sides…were they triggered into the most violent national confrontation in our history due to a genetic variant…or are we searching for an outcome to fit a notion?

The FBI concludes that most gang murders involve inner-city minority youth, and it does. The NIMH research is largely based on the

Department of Justice FBI model whereby barrios, ghettos and reservations seem to reproduce gangsters. Is it instead possible that these are negative sociological *outcomes* of a negative sociological process?

On its' face, this area of research seems reminiscent of **eugenics,** a widely accepted but inhumane belief structure and scientifically validated movement based on inhumane beliefs that translated to inhumane laws, policies and practices.

NIMH may be engaged in a search for neurobiological violence markers among *currently* high-violence groups that is no doubt inherent in the human animal, and which the triggering thereof has more to do with negative social, political, economic and environmental realities *that produce violent outcomes* than a predisposing violence gene, *a gene that every living creature likely possesses.*

These factors in-common should instead raise fundamental questions about the nature and relationship of community violence and/or peace *within a societal structure,* especially if there were common negative experiences emanating from the society of the aforementioned groups relative to the levels and types of violent reaction. Are there genetic similarities? Or is it more logical that the human animal *is predisposed* with an ability to become violent should he face extermination or otherwise be pushed hard and long enough to finally explode? People can and do become violent when threatened.

A better research question would ask what societal and environmental factors contribute to local conditions that bring out the violence potential in people.

The hundreds of thousands of Skinhead, Neo-Nazi, KKK gangs and their members historically engage in group violence. This is an interesting aspect in that they are *not* threatened by biased institutions, dehumanization, directed violence, exclusion or a "reservation" existence. They do purport to be "under invasion" and at risk of "losing" their homeland. These are some of the largest, most advanced, well-organized and identifiable violent gangs in US history yet not classified by NGC as

44

such (gang prerequisite: *turf, status and revenge*). They *do* have the prerequisites: a history, uniforms, leaders, turf (white America), graffiti and do band together to conduct illegal activities. Law enforcement reports that the fastest growing numbers of gang members are Caucasian/white. This "social/political movement" would seem eligible to be included in gang lists, jurisdictional injunctions and real research about community violence among groups.

One has to question what the objective is here…to solve the community violence problem or materialize a national scapegoat? By all appearances, the latter seems to have been accomplished. Selectively applied Draconian measures *are* the law of the land.

…and it just won't go away

There will probably always be those who attempt to prove an inherent one-upmanship of one group over others. The eugenics movement of last century sought to "prove" a scientific and biological superiority of the Anglo-Saxon white "race" over Latinos, Blacks, Jews, Eastern Europeans, American Indians, etc. Believers then used the vast powers almost exclusively available to them to advance eugenics in science, politics and academia with tragic results and lasting impact. Are we moving again in that direction?

As genetic violence marker theories and "early findings" continue to trigger premature and biased pronouncements, they lend unwarranted credibility to a belief construct based on certain groups suffering from inbred violent tendencies. If resorting to violence is thus "proven", it lends support to the NIMH premise that "peer influences" and "lapses in parenting" help trigger genetically predisposed youth to their violent calling. This could conceivably lead to "breakthrough" anti-gang medication for a Gang Deficit Disorder (GDD) to be administered to populations of minority young people fitting a particular *"well-researched" profile and residing in a "known gang breeding area".*

Such scientific "validations" also bolster social conditioning that gives the minority person a false sense of deficiency and inferiority and the majority child a false sense of innate superiority and worse: The KKK uses such "science" in their arguments to "send them back to Africa" and to Mexico, thus "cleansing" America of foreign influences and citing inbred violence disorders "proven" to be peculiar to minorities and according to "race".

Resorting to violence can result from an overload of anger and rage build-up as happened with the Colonists and indeed other groups in similar situations throughout world history. Did they suffer from "peer influences" and "lapses in parenting", too?

We can agree that any form of societal violence is not healthy. However, such violence does not just happen. Children are not born with a desire to kill and just need an opportunity to do so. Societal violence whether emanating from outside or from within indicates that deeper, more fundamental issues are involved, be it at the level of the individual, the group or a society. And violence begets violence. To want to kill your likeness for any reason should be considered signs of psychological damage and illness. To want to destroy members of an entire group is a major societal abnormality.

When the source or cause of a malady is unknown we are left to treat the symptoms. But do we ever stop searching?

If we use a standard medical disease model, we might follow a different course. To wit:

Disease: *A pathological condition of a system resulting from various causes and characterized by an identifiable group of signs or symptoms.*

If we consider that pathological violence is a disease, then we must look at the *host* and its *ecology, culture* and *environment,* the sub-systems and any and *all* other possible causes, sources and evolutionary processes *in addition to* the obvious *signs* and *symptoms.*

This model allows one to follow the evolution of community violence from contact with original pathogen through stages and to present day. This model encompasses processes of identification, analysis and interpretation, prescription and treatment and follows the results and outcomes of those prescriptions and treatments. The protocol allows the possibility of full examination of relationships between and among communities and a host society.

Each of these must be examined as part of this disease process especially as this disease is a killer of large numbers of future generations of identifiable groups of children within our society, and many others.

6

Social History and Violence

Countless reports, studies and lawsuits provide ample evidence of dehumanizing actions, cultural destruction and even ethnic cleansing aimed at the same groups that exhibit community and gang violence, a process that began soon after introduction.

Historical evidence depicts acts and policies detrimental to people of color by government, private institutions and citizens. These included violating basic freedoms beginning with the *right to life*…and the right to liberty and the pursuit of happiness. Lynching, rapes, indiscriminate murders, thefts of land and more were perpetrated by citizens against original indigenous inhabitants, against those enslaved and other people of color.

Lawful, properly ordered laws and policies were enacted whose effect was to begin and sustain a process of absolute power and control that included subjugation, physical displacement and outright removal of groups. They were excluded in social planning except as commodities. These acts and policies *preceded* the emergence of a community's gangs.

It would seem logical that over time and negative experiences groups would eventually begin to experience collective outrage and become at increased risk of volatility along with a lowering of their violence threshold. Groups with the most chronic violence issues suffered similarly severe experiences in this regard (Native Americans, Latinos and African-

Americans). Nations that experience group violence by gangs and other forms of collective reactionary rage share comparable social histories, e.g., Australia, United Kingdom, Ireland, France, Germany, Spain, South Africa and others.

The term "race" as a social construct was developed in Germany in the 1700's. This forever established the elevation of white persons over non-white persons and underpins all manner of societal dysfunction. When groups are relegated to a descending classification system (race) and institutionally classified and treated accordingly, the diminishing of personhood is complete. This belief construct reduced select groups using popular demeaning, mistreatment and restrictive laws, policies and reduced freedoms. And some were not considered human. Groups were dehumanized in word, thought and deed. It is important to understand the scope of the term, "dehumanize": *to deprive of human qualities.* They were *not* considered children of an almighty God.

The Circle of Science, Racism and Violence

Depopulation and management of groups is a messy business. And dehumanization is a two way road to social destruction. As we learned from the tragedy of the Holocaust, dehumanization of targeted groups in the eyes of the general population is a necessary first step in people removal and elimination. But the entire process can be overwhelming to the system and to those charged with executing a society's program. In this way, dehumanization affects the oppressor as well as the oppressed.

To dehumanize, one must lose focus, meaning and significance of *humanity.* It is a slippery slope when playing in God's domain.

And the disposal of the end-product is rarely if ever thought out. Ovens, reservations and prisons have at times become overwhelmed by sheer numbers and enormous operational costs, even though various forms of genocide as a final solution have been tried, overtly and covertly.

Let us review how Nazi Germany was able to get so far in maintaining that their form of eugenics was the correct way to deal with undesirable groups. Groups were portrayed as sub-human and genetically challenged; as naturally violent, freeloaders on social resources, criminally inclined, illegal substance peddlers and abusers, unskilled, uneducated, unemployed lawbreakers and even cold-blooded killers.

These "minorities" were structurally uneducated and unemployable and placed in ghettos. It was logical to systematically and structurally leave them out of political, social and economic involvement and productive social endeavors. They were herded onto "reservations" with enough to subsist. They became an unwieldy drag on societal resources. Nazis then chose an option that took the argument to its logical end.

Had they chosen another, less overt option they may have been less successful at reaching a final solution but would have likely evolved a social, economic and political system much like our own.

It also seems conceivable that at some tipping point, representative numbers would begin to rebel, to behave badly, sufficient to confirm the negative propaganda, thus allowing ever-harsher "management" plans to move forward with acquiescence from a demanding citizenry and an understanding world. Nazis could manage and control groups now effectively corralled into "reservations" and make careers and profit on the growing *prison industrial complex* demanded by this scheme. And rather than public revulsion, enjoy the public's vehement support.

Even so, the resources needed to maintain such a containment and disposal process would eventually be overwhelmed.

Our leaders used massacres, purposeful spreading of killer-diseases, starvation, death marches, lynching, burning alive, dragging to death, murder, robbery, rape, imprisonment, resource depravation and deportation and while media and other institutions instill and reinforce a negative belief structure aimed at undesirable populations, thus "educating" the masses about their undesirability and to rationalize terrorist behavior.

Those that work in these environments would have to believe in the unworthiness of their charges or risk suffering a dehumanized existence as well. They do see the "disease" at its most advanced stages so separation is possible.

Some will always maintain members of some groups are sub-human, genetically challenged, naturally violent, a drag on social resources, criminally inclined, illegal substance peddlers and abusers, unskilled, uneducated, unemployed lawbreakers and cold-blooded killers. In our situation the targeted populations have bought the nightmare and adopted it as their own. The "client" at this stage may exhibit a kind of death of spirit mixed with explosive fury that validates such "management".

Turning science on its head

The "science" of *eugenics* evolved methods to enhance breeding of "fit" white persons and restrict breeding of "unfit" non-white persons, including forced sterilization. From 1910 to the 1940's, this belief system was especially strong in the United States, England and Germany where *eugenics* had leaders and followers in the scientific, political and religious establishments and academia (http://en.wikipedia.org/wiki/Eugenics).

Nazi Germany attempted to take this belief system to its logical end with disastrous results.

At about the same time, in America, 24 states passed sterilization laws and 30 states had laws aimed at social "misfits" of color along with the retarded, criminals and the insane. Many states passed laws prohibiting mixed-race marriages and the federal 1924 Immigration Act (termed National Origins Act) severely limited those who could come to this country for fear of polluting the Anglo-Saxon population.

Scientific evidence now shows *no such genetic racial distinction exists among humans,* and in fact, the opposite is true: when following genetic origins of persons of different "races", there have been found closer genetic relationships between some black and white persons than of those that were the same color.

Recent findings in genetic research validate that *there is no scientific support for "race" as a biological determiner or trait; that there may be at most genetic variants that distinguish skin color, eye or hair color* (Adelman, Larry, **Race - The Power of an Illusion,** PBS, 2003*).* "Race" as a biological basis of human distinction is specious. "Race" is nothing more than a human construct - a concept and nothing else. As true genetic research unfolds, similarities will likely replace differences.

The "science" of *eugenics* is now in disrepute but the belief system that brought it into being stubbornly remains. According to Adelman, *"a belief in biological race also obscures the very salient consequences of race as learned experience. Race may be a biological myth, a social construction, but it nonetheless remains very real. It can even have biological effects.*

African-Americans have among the highest rates of hypertension in the world. This was long assumed to be genetic, a "marker" of their nature. But then it was found that West Africans have among the world's lowest hypertension rates.

A focus of race, as innate biology, as genetic difference, would lead health professionals and policymakers to overlook social factors that might contribute to African American hypertension and heart disease, including the added stressor of living in a racist society".

Adelman continued…

"Race is terribly relevant to life outcomes. The likelihood that toxic waste has been dumped in your neighborhood, your ability to get a home loan, the quality of your kids education, connections to job opportunities, whether or not you are likely to be followed in a department store or pulled over by police, are all influenced by your race. Race does matter. Not race as genetics, but what sociologists call "social" race. Social race is an important variable for health researchers and epidemiologists." (Adelman, Larry, **Race - The Power of an Illusion,** PBS, 2003*).*

Race as currently defined, is not an indicator of success or failure, achievement, violence or anything else. However, race has been used when allocating resources that would help determine achievement and success or hopelessness and failure. "Race" has been used as a method to contain, withhold freedoms and benefits and then monitor "social failures" claiming some "races" inherently "underperform" other "races". This usage also supports a false belief of group superiority and inferiority... especially to children on both sides of a made-up scale. The term "race" must refer to and be associated with its intended use: unjustified marginalization, discrimination, dehumanization, bias and exclusion...all negative connotations emanating from its existence. It is time to turn the page on "race".

Popular belief has guided research which helped establish guidelines that became policies and laws carried out by institutions which negatively affected the lives of people of color and culture, and continued to guide and reinforce popular belief for each new generation. *And children adapt to them.* Members of non-white groups will often nod to each other in acknowledgment of their common (negative) status in society and all that it means. Science must be mindful not to allow bad assumptions lay groundwork for further separation, containment, control and manipulation of easily identifiable groups, *based on a set of beliefs.*

We can never know all there is to know about the enslaving, raping and murdering of African-Americans, Asians, Mexican Americans and Native Americans but we do know that these groups have these as shared experiences. During this nation's history, the abuse and killing of these groups for sport or practiced belief was allowed; as were destruction of cultural and religious icons, illegal deportations and imprisonment; and the rounding up and placing of groups on desolate reservations by various means including forced death marches were government policy. These actions and more were designed to benefit the majority group and had an impact on both sides: one elevated in wealth and position and the other systematically decimated.

Government establishes the original "affirmative action"

Property redlining began in the 1930's when the federal government created subsidized low-cost home loans to spur home ownership and growth. The United States Bureau of the Census in partnership with the Federal Housing Administration established a national appraisal system that mapped where minority families lived. Restrictive lending policies for such mixed neighborhoods were then established while granting favorable loan treatment and generous redevelopment grants to all-white neighborhoods. *(Marc Seitles, "The Perpetuation of Residential Racial Segregation in America: Historical Discrimination. Modern Forms of Exclusion and Illusionary Remedies" © 1996 Journal of Land Use & Environmental Law).*

The U.S. Census thus directed where taxpayer supported funding would flow for community resource infrastructure development including favorable financing for homes, schools, libraries, parks, museums and playgrounds.

These policies also established a favorable institutional framework for banking, insurance and retail investment for decades to come. This extended to awarding of educational grants, government contracts and jobs. Imagine this nation today if all groups and communities benefitted from such favorable treatment. "Disorganized communities" would not exist today. Multi-$Billions of everyone's tax dollars have been dedicated to the improvement, health and wealth of the majority group in various government giveaways as a matter of course.

The 1790 Naturalization Act permitted only "free white persons" to become naturalized citizens, further restricting non-white access to citizenship and government largess; the landmark Social Security Act of 1935 excluded agricultural and domestic workers who were mostly Asian, Americans of Mexican descent and African-American; the 1935 Wagner Act allowed persons to unionize but allowed unions to exclude non-whites; the Supreme Court rulings of 1857 and 1896 respectively, affirmed slavery and the constitutionality of racial segregation.

In the decade from 1929 to 1940, close to one-half million American citizens of Mexican descent since before the Southwest was part of the USA were deported to Mexico losing their homes, lands and businesses. U.S. Immigration with local law enforcement burst into homes with guns drawn and did not let families take anything, including birth certificates and other documents that would prove citizenship.

During World War II, Asians were lawfully interned and lost their homes, lands and businesses. A century earlier the 1830 Indian Removal Act allowed for the forcible relocation of tribes to make way for white settlers who were then given the land free under the 1862 Homestead Act.

Entire populations have been systematically excluded from participation in acts of selective distribution except as "donors" through taxes or as former owners of lands, homes and businesses taken without compensation or recourse and at the cost of livelihoods, liberties and lives. These policies helped the majority population accumulate the wealth, position and power they enjoy today. There were no outcries on the Senate floor of the unconstitutionality of it, the unfairness of using everyone's tax dollars to help purchase homes, improve education, health and wealth for a select few.

Lawsuits and legislation that attempt to put in place even a modicum of similar benefits or to help groups that were left out of the government munificence have found difficult going. These efforts are termed "favoritism", "preferential treatment", "reverse racism", "socialism" and even communism and have been used to denigrate simply by their mention. Affirmative Action, parity and set-asides for minority individuals and businesses are policies that have been given a negative connotation in messages generated by biased politicians and spokespersons and carried throughout the land by a compliant media. These policies are referred to in a ways that further demean those who attempt to make use of them by making them feel "less than" for even considering such assistance. Today, such parity programs are almost non-existent, victims of white backlash. The full story is not told so cannot be factored in to people's thinking.

In actuality, all the affirmative action programs ever imagined would not match the government benefits given the majority population to ensure their success. And whether by force or by edict, the entire process amounts to violence done against particular groups to benefit a select group. How these deeds are labeled and presented by media shapes the way the general population accepts or rejects them.

The battle still rages between those who would continue to subvert fair and equal opportunity and withhold well earned steps to prosperity and those who would level the playing field. Be mindful that a society cannot move forward while driving backward…and cannot call itself civilized while behaving in an uncivilized manner. The uninvited may just spoil the party.

As we progress into our third century, education funding is still woefully unequal. We continue to uncover acts, policies and patterns of bias in housing, employment, lending and judicial processes. When one becomes familiar with the vast breadth and scope of the favoritism/discrimination paradigm, one cannot help but reach the conclusion that part of this nation's successful 225 year march entailed overt and covert maneuverings and exclusion of some of us to attain success for others. Biased acts and policies continue to be upheld and preserved by God-fearing American citizens – those elected, appointed and employed. Human nature must sometimes be protected from itself. Lord, help us.

For more than three centuries Native Americans, African-Americans, Latinos, Asians, Jews, Irish, Poles, Italians and others have had to overcome hate crimes, discriminatory laws, policies and practices, and terrorist acts and behaviors in the United States of America and many of these groups evolved gangs and some rioted. ***But a causative connection between gangs and other abnormally elevated levels of community violence and violent social histories in-common had not been made…until now.***

7

It Takes a Nation to Raise a Gangster...

...the **Reservation Community Syndrome**

The Native American experience is one that is rarely highlighted in commentaries about American racism. A stunning action by the United States Department of the Interior's Bureau of Indian Affairs provides a dramatic and instructive object lesson:

At the ceremony honoring the Bureau's 175th anniversary, held September 8, 2000, Kevin Gover, Assistant Secretary of Indian Affairs issued a formal apology to Native Americans for acts against these first Americans. He said in part: "this agency at various times profoundly harmed the communities it was meant to serve…it was an instrument…to execute the removal of…tribal nations." That, "this agency participated in ethnic cleansing that befell the western tribes"; engaged in "death marches" and "the deliberate spread of disease, the decimation of herds, the use of the poison alcohol to destroy mind and body, and the cowardly killing of women and children (that) made for a tragedy on a scale so ghastly that cannot be dismissed".

He spoke of the "destructive efforts to annihilate Indian cultures" and the "devastation of Tribal economies" and "forced dependence on this agency". He also pointed out how "thefts of land" and how the government agency "forbade Indian languages, religious activities, governments and made Indian people ashamed of who they were" were activities that required an apology. And "worst of all," he stated, "the Bureau...committed these acts against the children entrusted to its boarding schools, brutalizing them emotionally, psychologically, physically and spiritually." He added, "The trauma of shame, fear and anger has passed from one generation to the next, and manifests itself in rampant alcoholism, suicides and violent deaths at the hands of one another".

He spoke of "dehumanization and purposeful stereotyping them as sub-human, leading American people to shallow and ignorant beliefs about Indians." And who "in the past has committed acts so terrible that they affect, diminish, and destroy the lives of Indian people decades later, generations later." Alas, there it is: dehumanization, ethnic cleansing and genocide, cultural destruction: *terrorism*...and the multi-generational consequences thereof.

It was a bold first step toward acknowledging blame for past practices that reverberates today. As it turns out this first step was short-lived. Even so, in the same year the Catholic Church made a similar gesture of apology to indigenous peoples in the Americas. And on June 4, 2005 a memorial to the Navajo Long Walk was dedicated in New Mexico. The Lieutenant Governor stated that it is a dark chapter in our nation's history, referring to the reservation as a brutal prison camp.

These statements emanating from the United States government, the Catholic Church and one state in the union are profound. I encourage you to read the preceding paragraphs again as they exemplify how and why an otherwise healthy and vibrant people can devolve to become unstable and eventually self-destructive, all resulting from a society's beliefs, policies, laws and behaviors directed at them.

Native American nations have been brutally contained and horrifically managed. As stated by Assistant Secretary Gover, the results of such societal "management" are foundational to Native American's ongoing deleterious mental, physical and emotional existence and continued deterioration. And as crime rates rise and fall in other parts of this country, reservations continue to become more dangerous for native youth. According to a Department of Justice study, of the 550 recognized tribes, their youth ages 12-20 are 58% more likely to be crime victims than whites and blacks; those under 15 are murdered at twice the rate of white teenagers, commit suicide at more than twice the rate of non-Native American youth, suffer from alcohol related deaths at more than 10 times and are arrested for alcohol related crimes at twice the national average. The study also found that school failure rates are much higher than those found in the rest of society. And they are not alone. For even as youth mortality rates might ebb and flow in some communities, here they remain in a deadly spiral.

The *other* model neighborhood: the *"reservation community"*

It is appropriate to view the Native American experience as applicable to thousands of communities in cities and towns across this great nation where minority families have had to overcome comparable adversity. There are glaring similarities between communities on urban "reservations" and those of the Native American and regardless of geography the outcomes are too similar to dismiss as ethnic or genetic peculiarities. In the wake of America's social history are Native American reservations and urban "reservations" spread out across America. Young people in each "reservation", regardless of location, culture or ethnicity inherit the tragic past of those gone before, and is where a people, now subdued, end up under government control and supervision. This is where fear, distrust of "outsiders" and institutions, hopelessness and fatalism manifests…and the crimson flow continues to spread.

The Reservation Community Syndrome: *the widespread and prolonged subjecting of a particular group(s) to physical, social, economic and political adversity and the consequent in-group(s) frustration, anger, rage, aggression and violence patterns.*

A society can manipulate social, economic and political elements to support, enhance and maintain one segment, to the detriment of other segments. Over time, the process becomes traditional and entails a system of violence and violations of human and civil rights resulting in an aberrant societal manifestation: the "reservation community".

. These are communities where groups are cut off from traditional social and government munificence and survive straddling second and third-world conditions. The classic "reservation community" experiences physical, economic, political, social and religious societal violence that debilitates and weakens the very heart and soul of home and community. We read about but can never fully fathom the damage caused by slavery, land theft, illegal deportation and segregation. The screams and taunts followed by being thrown out of places you helped build. And the redlining of all sorts, the prison camps and other forms of round-ups, withholding of voting rights, outlawing of religions, etc., etc., etc.

The more visible activities reads like psychopaths run amok: shooting galleries using live targets, mass murder, dragging to death, dismembering and skinning alive, lynching, burning, gang raping, tar and feathering and more. If terrorism is defined as acts designed to place fear in the hearts and minds of a population, then these indeed rank with the worst acts of terrorism.

Every minority group in the United States of America has suffered some of these. They ingested the societal violence and turned frustration, grief and anger inward rather than attack a country they want desperately to be part of.

Over time, elements of an affected community adjust by adopting negative social modifications in order to satisfy basic needs. These reinforce already negative beliefs about their group among the general population *and* among their own resulting in increased group isolation and control and collective negative self-image. Violence patterns emerge that further degrades local conditions justifying added controls and containment. Once the process becomes institutionalized, violence "root causes" are seemingly apparent but ignored.

Consider the following statements:

62

➢ The "reservation community" is the quintessence of the American experience that racial and ethnic groups have endured and continue to endure.

➢ The "reservation community" experience is in its essence elevated unrest and upheaval emanating from external sources.

➢ Such ongoing and relentless violence aimed en masse at such group's physical, emotional and psychic being, can result in abnormal reactive behaviors, the most immediately noticed is violence done to self and those close.

➢ The violent reactions can be viewed as *outcomes* of such external violence or be used to confirm the group's ongoing negative treatment.

➢ Societal violence against a people is at the root, *the origin* of what has evolved to become elevated levels of "reservation community" destruction and self-eliminating violence.

An analogy would be relocating an ethnic group on an island with a regimen of potentially deadly bacteria and without concern for possible outcomes. Eventually the numbers of persons that become ill and die increase. As elevating numbers become widely noticed, explain the deadly "disease" phenomenon is endemic to the island population, it's in their DNA. Or they catch it from their role models. But indeed, all agree something must be done!

Forces are sent to the island with a "treatment" program of resource and economic deprivation, negative belief management and institutional supervision and controls. As the "illness" remains rampant, the dosage is increased and punitive measures are added for "reactionaries". Media joins the PR messaging arsenal. After a time, officials claim the "islanders" are unresponsive to treatment in spite of Herculean efforts and millions of dollars stating, "We have to give up on this generation and concentrate on the next". By now, the "treatment" modality has expanded to include island parents and newborns.

Researchers are enlisted and go to great lengths to count the dead and dying, noting how many different ways they become ill and expire. They become part of the many economic enterprises that have mushroomed around the island.

"Treatment" has become a symbiotic maintenance program relying on re-infection of youthful "islander" populations from birth.

On our island "reservation communities", simple cures for the original and once uncomplicated bacterial infection are never tried as identifying it would reveal the original malevolent act.

Meanwhile, the bacteria mutate and escape creating concern for public safety on the non-infected "mainland". Researchers explain that coming in contact may cause temporarily illness but recovery is imminent. They do caution against too much exposure. The infecting bacteria continue to be ignored at the expense of the original infected group. Institutions now insist the origin and intransigence of the disease is with that island group; they are the problem and must be dealt with accordingly.

This explanation becomes the core belief about "reservation community" "islanders" throughout the rest of society.

In "reservation communities", or, "disorganized communities" if you like, the original violence "infecting bacteria" have not been described accurately to this day. Such social "pathogens" have origin and evolution but only violent outcomes are examined.

The Human Genome and the epigenome

The concept that persons in certain barrios, ghettos and indeed Native American reservations share a "reservation community" existence that passes from generation to generation has scientific support. One area of study undergoing intellectual development helps explain the process of intergenerational transmission of shared trauma. *Massive group trauma, Historical Trauma (HT), multi-generational trauma and intergenerational trauma* are terms that help describe a process that is not dissimilar to what survivors of the Holocaust and their descendants experienced.

Columnists Roberto Rodriguez and Patrisia Gonzales have long addressed humanitarian issues in their Column of the Americas (XColumn@gmail.com). In one such column, Patrisia writes about Dr. Karina Walters, A noted Choctaw scholar who points out that the trauma is targeted at the collective and to the collective experience but is held personally and transmitted individually over generations. Thus, she states, even family members who have not directly experienced the trauma can feel the effects of the event(s) generations later as proffered in the BIA apology. Patrisia also writes of Dr. Maria Yellow Horse Brave Heart, who has advanced the concept of Historical Trauma (HT).

This work illuminates the way in which indigenous scholars are examining evolutionary processes to better understand how violence eventuates within a community from the outside in *before* it manifests *within,* especially as intra-community violence. The extensive apology made by the BIA helps establish links within the Native American chain of violence in an area that is certainly applicable to others with similar experience. This universe of deleterious experience is shared by sister "reservation communities" past and present e.g. African-Americans, Latino/ Hispanic Americans, Asian-Americans and other minorities in this country and certainly in other countries.

The exploration of genetics and behaviours appear to validate the theory of multigenerational / Historical Trauma.

DNA is not the be-all of human behaviour: *"A genome is the complete set of deoxyribonucleic acid, or DNA, in a cell. DNA carries the instructions for building all of the proteins that make each living creature unique. Derived from the Greek, epigenome means "above" the genome. The epigenome consists of chemical compounds that modify, or mark, the genome in a way that tells it what to do, where to do it and when to do it. The marks, which are not part of the DNA itself, can be passed on from cell to cell as cells divide and from one generation to the next."* **(**http://www.genome.gov/27532724**).**

Epigenetic tagging actually "guides" the human genome in behavior and other aspects that help shape the person. This new research illustrates that certain epigenetic tags *may be more likely* to be activated in affected persons as response to social ecology that involves traumatic experiences of various types, levels and durations. Epigenetics can make identical twins not identical even though they have the same genetic make-up.

Research is mainly concerned with relevance to diseases at this point. However, in the search for causes and solutions to violence, research can and should expand to include social histories and the degree or severity of social, physical, emotional and even economic impact on a people and/or group. Past can and does impact the future but not due to genetic abnormalities as some propose but rather due to group social history.

The following excerpts are from an APA (American Psychological Association) special report entitled, "Psychological Treatment of Ethnic Minority Persons" by the Council of National Psychological Associations for the Advancement of Ethnic Minority Interests.

The group consists of The Asian American Psychological Association (AAPA), The Association of Black Psychologists (ABPsi), The National Latina/o Psychological Association (NLPA) and The Society of Indian Psychologists (SIP) and published by the Association of Black Psychologists, Washington, D.C., 11/2003. The report discusses psychological well-being and treatment considerations as seen by treating professionals from each group. It is interesting that common concerns, experiences and outcomes are evident throughout the report to the point that the groups are almost interchangeable.

From the report:

As re: <u>Asian Americans</u>: *"Historically, racism and sexism toward Asian Americans and Pacific Islanders in the United States have been prevalent. Whether mandated by U.S. Government (e. g., Gentleman's Agreement of 1860, anti-miscegenation laws, and unconstitutional internment of Japanese Americans during World War II) or acted upon by individuals via hate crimes, Asian Americans and Pacific Islanders continue to face oppression and racism in the United States. For any Asian Americans and Pacific Islanders, the sense of collectivism and group identity results in a shared experience of discrimination,*

66

even when such events are experienced by other Asian Americans and Pacific Islanders.

Psychological researchers have documented the effects of trans-generational psychological trauma among Asian Americans and Pacific Islanders. For example, children of Japanese Americans interned during WW II experienced negative psychological sequelae from the internment. The concept of trans generational trauma also is particularly important given the large number of Asian Americans and Pacific Islanders who have immigrated to the United States from countries ravaged by war, famine, and economic and political upheaval. Although their progeny may not have personally been tortured, raped, or beaten, their parents who did experience those atrocities may pass down the psychological trauma to them. Many Asian Americans and Pacific Islanders are regularly bombarded with messages to assimilate and that their culture and heritage are not valued.

A specific example is the English-only initiative. Rather than valuing multilingual individuals as an important resource, several states have had English-only initiatives that could be interpreted as intolerance and non-acceptance for individuals who speak languages other than English. These initiatives are typically generated by European Americans who lack the ability to speak other languages as well as knowledge of the future potential economic growth and resources of the population they purport to represent. An interesting irony is that a century ago, European Americans prevented non-English speaking minorities from learning English for fear they would become educated and compete economically. Although the most frequently spoken languages in the world are Asian, the U.S. education system places more value on European-based languages over Asian languages, creating yet another barrier. This is most readily observed by examining the foreign language offerings in most middle schools, high schools, colleges, and universities. This results in fewer individuals having the capability to communicate with Asian American/Pacific Islander immigrants whose first language is Asian, which, in turn, affects the number of treatment providers who can provide services in clients' first language. When employed, Asian Americans and Pacific Islanders continue to experience the glass-ceiling effect. Although trained and competent, in many companies, Asian Americans and Pacific Islanders find it difficult to move beyond mid level positions. Stereotypes of Asian American/Pacific Islander employees of being smart, hardworking, and reliable, yet passive and quiet, result in many individuals being passed over for much-deserved promotions and recognition. Implications for negative effects on self-worth are clear. Negative stereotypes of Asian American/Pacific Islander men being undesirable, while stereotypes of Asian American/Pacific Islander women as exotic and sexualized are also psychologically damaging. A damaging result of the model minority myth is that many Asian Americans/Pacific Islanders are invisible minorities. This is particularly the case when discussions of diversity focus only on "Black/White" issues..." By Gayle Y. Iwamasa, PhD, Asian American Psychological Association.

As re: <u>African-Americans</u>, the implications are similar to other group's experiences: *"For example, a history of enslavement, colonization, and neocolonialism is the foundation for current state of affairs throughout the African world. This state of affairs can impact symptom formation in a number of critical ways. One of the most common is the adoption of the beliefs and values of the dominant group to the detriment of one's own self and collective group, below are three examples.*

• ***Identification with the aggressor**—taking on the beliefs, values and behaviors of the oppressor, trying to be "more like" the oppressor, than the oppressor, manifesting in a anti-self disorder in which "the other" and his/her characteristics are perceived more desirable that one's own and there is no knowledge of one's own outside of the interpretation and con text of "the other"*

• ***Internalized oppression**--anger, rage, and sense of inferiority and self-loathing turned inward, manifest in anti- self and alien–self disorders in which on acts in way detrimental to self and one's group of origin (e. g., willingness to play role of "overseer," or gatekeeper to block progress of member's of one's own group)*

• ***Attempts to escape** the perpetual mini assaults and major life traumas of racism and white supremacy through psychotic escape, substance abuse, black-on-black crime, and suicidal behavior or homicide..."*

And continuing: *"...Starting with African Americans whose immigration to America was forced, and whose labor netted this nation – and most of Western European nation s – the economic dominance they have enjoyed for centuries, the group is unique by virtue of the nature, quality, and degree of socially sanctioned violence, hostility, and aggression practiced by the dominant culture towards them generation after generation. At the same time, it is imperative to understand that their "beingness" is not limited to a reactionary navigation through foreign inhumane circumstances and conditions forced upon them. The resilience of this cultural group is astounding in the face of the non-stop negating onslaught from the dominant culture.*

As the formal mechanisms of cultural transmission remain under attack, disruption of the group's own indigenous strengths continue to be apparent. Those given opportunity typically flourish and often excel, according to the dominant cultural standards. Those most disenfranchised economically and educationally, may also experience the "good life," a life of peace, joy, and well-being, depending on their relationship to traditional African values and beliefs. Those who seek access, whether or not they may "get in" to the non-merit based system of material rewards offered by the dominant culture, also suffer, as they often internalize oppression and succumb to psychological incarceration..." By Linda James Myers, PhD; Anthony Young, PsyD; Ezemenari Obasi, MA, Suzette Speight, PhD, Association of Black Psychologists.

As re: **Latino/Hispanics:** *"The underutilization of mental health services by Hispanics in the United States is deeply rooted in White America's refusal to recognize and value the central role of Hispanics in the past, present, and future of this country. The educational, political, and economic development of Hispanics has been characterized by a history of neglect, oppression, and long periods of passive if not deliberate denial of opportunity. While overt racism is no longer acceptable in many areas of modern American society, subtle and more overt vestiges of oppression and racism continue linguistically, educationally, and economically:*

Language: *A young child who speaks English as well as a second language such as German, French, or Italian is viewed as precocious. In contrast, many children who speak English and Spanish are considered deficient.*

Education: *Not only are a disproportionate number of Latino students placed into special education programs but districts with higher proportions of White teachers enroll minorities in special education at a higher rate.*

Economic: *Many Hispanics earn very low wages because of low levels of educational attainment. However, Latino high school and college graduates earn less than their White and African American counterparts.*

In addition, undocumented immigrants often live in extreme density conditions and may be exploited, working at the most difficult and undesirable jobs for less than minimum wage and at times not paid for their labor by unscrupulous contractors." By Andres Barona, PhD; Maryann Santos de Barona, PhD, National Latina/o Psychological Association

And as re: <u>Native Americans</u>: *"The history of the Native American includes the invasion of European immigrants, loss of the war effort to keep their land, forced removal of Native people of the eastern United States to the Oklahoma area, confinement of Native people to reservations, decimation of the population by diseases such as smallpox, disruption of Native culture by constant fighting and moving, religious persecution, and introduction of alcohol. In the early 1800s, the policy of the U.S. government was to kill or remove Native people from their historic homelands in the eastern United States to accommodate the growing need for land by European settlers. The Native people were cheated, tricked, and forced to move, and many died of cold, disease, and starvation during these moves. This Indian removal effort is known to Natives as the "trails of tears" because of the deep sorrow experienced by the Native people who lost their land and loved ones. During this 400-year period in their history, numerous Native people died, and traditional Native culture was severely disrupted. The 1900s were a period of recovery, with tribes seeking to maintain their traditional ways under the constant pressure of acculturation stressors and the need to survive and thrive in the "modern" world.*

Two major cultural genocide efforts further disrupted and complicated the recovery of Native people during the 1900s, Indian boarding schools and the Indian Relocation Program. The boarding schools were a forced education and Christianizing effort by the U.S. government and various churches to change the "heathen" and uneducated Native people into "civilized" and Christian citizens. Children were forcibly taken from their homes and placed in government or church boarding schools, their hair was cut, they were put in uniforms, beaten if caught speaking their language or practicing their own ways, and they were not allowed visits from their families or visits to their homes.

An entire generation of Native people was subjected to this treatment, and the extent and severity of the abuse suffered by these children is still being uncovered and still affecting their offspring.

The effects of the boarding schools have been far reaching and intergenerational in their impact on American Indian people. The generation of Native people who were subjected to this atrocity experienced a loss of their culture and a loss of the opportunity to learn parenting skills.

Because of the severe physical and sexual abuse perpetrated upon these unprotected and captive Native children, as adults, they have experienced depression, anxiety, and post traumatic stress disorders, as well as some of them becoming perpetrators of abuse themselves. In addition, many of these Native people turned to drugs and alcohol to cope with the pain they were experiencing.

The Indian Relocation Program was part of an effort in the 1960s to do away with American Indian reservations. Native people on the reservation were offered travel assistance and funding support to leave the reservations and move to large cities (Los Angeles, Chicago, Denver, and others) to find a job and settle there. These large cities still have large populations of American Indian people who have remained there and are now "urban Indians" as opposed to "reservation Indians." The effect of the Indian Relocation Program was not to abolish reservations but to create Indian ghettos in large cities and to further disrupt the culture. Many of these Native people became "marginalized," meaning that they no longer fit into their own cultural group nor were they part of the majority population. Thus, they were, basically, without a culture. Their children grew up distanced from their extended family and their culture, perhaps visiting only during the summers and likely not speaking their native language, while simultaneously experiencing discrimination from the majority culture.

American Indians are the only minority group in the United States that has a legal definition of their race (.25blood quantum).This method is used to determine eligibility for services. Not all Native people recognize the federal government definition, and asking, "How much Indian are you?" would be an inappropriate and insensitive question to ask a Native person. Over 150 Indian languages are still used, and there are elders who still speak only their own language. Native tradition is an oral one, with history and stories passed down orally. Only within the 1900s did most Native tribes begin to try to develop a written language. Because of this, very few Native people can read or write in their own language.

Unemployment on American Indian reservations is consistently high, ranging from 80% in some plains states to 20% in more prosperous tribes. The poverty rate is quite high and similar to those of African American and Hispanic people. It is reported that nearly one third of all American Indian adults are functionally illiterate, and those 25 years and older have an average of 9.6 years of formal education. This is below the 10.9 year national mean and is the lowest of any ethnic minority group in the nation. On a more encouraging note, in the fall of 1996, 134,000 American Indians were enrolled in the nation's colleges and universities, up from 84,000 in the fall of 1980. During the 1995-1996 school year, about 15,000 of the nation's American Indians and Alaska Natives received college degrees.

In the face of very difficult times, American Indian people have demonstrated extraordinary strength, and many have found healthy ways of coping with the stress of forced acculturation, attempted genocide, loss of land and culture, and the death of loved ones. They have coped by practicing Native spirituality, valuing connections with families and communities, and initiating a grassroots movement toward healthier life styles. Unfortunately, all these stressors have taken their toll on American Indian and Alaskan Native people.

Depression and adjustment reactions are the most prevalent mental health problems, with suicide among adults more than twice as high as rates in the majority culture, and in school-age children 3 times greater than that of White Americans.

A congressional hearing on Native juvenile alcoholism and drug abuse reported that 52% of urban Indian adolescents and 80% of reservation Indian adolescents engaged in heavy alcohol or drug use compared to 23% of their urban, non-Indian counterparts. Delinquency and arrest rates are the highest of any ethnic minority group. Because of alcohol problems and family disruption, child abuse is also a problem in some tribes." By Carolyn Barcus, EdD Society of Indian Psychologists

*

These communities exhibit higher rates of self-destructive behavior than the norm. However, incidents of self-destructive behavior for Native Americans are higher than other groups. All suffered extraordinary multi-generational trauma and the BIA apology relating to Native Americans could easily fit the other groups. Each suffered indiscriminate murders and had land and property stolen from them. The Native American's higher rates may indicate an earlier onset and longer duration of trauma(s); an elevated level of trauma (more concentrated and comprehensive); a continuing relatively lower social, economic and political standing; or all three and more that carefully directed research would help uncover to then find solutions and cures.

Humans react in similar ways to similar stimuli

Although there may be minor differences as to how particular groups respond to similar trauma, the evidence suggests that traumatic conditions and influences underlie each. The violent and self-destructive actions exhibited by the affected groups are too similar to dismiss as behavior "typical of minorities" without investigating the society as common denominator. Or, we would have to accept the existence of another common denominator such as a gene peculiar to ethnic/minority people capable of producing gangs and the like or at least a "predisposing heritable trait" as stated by the National Institute of Mental Health (NIMH).

If this area of study remains so circumscribed, NIMH should indeed search for a genetic predisposition among groups for propensity to engage in slavery, murder, rape, land theft, dehumanization and attempted genocide.

The experience of each minority group that has evolved violent youth groups has been the same. "Reservation communities" are created by the same forces regardless of society or group, and with time and experience, people living in those "reservations" will follow similar reactive patterns.

Maintaining national innocence or acknowledging national disgrace

PBS recently presented "Mark Twain", based on his life and his travels in later years. I noted how Samuel Clemens, AKA Mark Twain, commented on how vicious and barbaric enslavement and 'murder for sport' based on race was juxtaposed with the purveyor's belief in a "national innocence". He wrote of the brutal enslavement of native peoples by Europeans in furtherance of their fortunes. He saw this repeated from Australia to South Africa and the Congo and the United States of America. His ongoing commentary was an observation of man's inhumanity to man and his feeble attempts to justify the unjustifiable.

On another PBS show, <u>Bill Moyers Journal</u>, (PBS), Dr. James Cone, an accomplished author and religious theologian reflected on the fallacy of the concept of "national innocence". He also spoke of the missing impact of theologian Reinhold Niebuhr, whose 20th century work related theology to modern society and politics. In 2005, famed historian Arthur Schlesinger Jr. lamented the disappearance of Niebuhr from modern discourse:

"...maybe Niebuhr has fallen out of fashion because 9/11 has revived the myth of our national innocence. Lamentations about "the end of innocence" became favorite clichés at the time. Niebuhr was a critic of national innocence, which he regarded as a delusion. After all, whites coming to these shores were reared in the Calvinist doctrine of sinful humanity, and they killed red men, enslaved black men and later on imported yellow men for peon labor - not much of a background for national innocence. Nations, as individuals, who are completely innocent in their own esteem," Niebuhr wrote, "are insufferable in their human contacts." The self-righteous delusion of innocence encouraged a kind of Manichaeism dividing the world between good (us) and evil (our critics)."

And later on the same show, a revelation of collective violent behavior "innocently" pursued:

"The work of historian and photographer Ken Gonzales-Day documents the lost history of lynching and reminds Americans that not all lynching took place in the South and that Native Americans, Chinese immigrants, and Latinos were also victims of the (white) lynch mob. His photograph of a "Hang Tree" in California begins the slideshow." (www.pbs.org/moyers/journal/11232007/profile.html; dnld: 11/25/07). *"In fact, Gonzales-Day was able to document 350 lynchings in the State of California between 1850 and 1935. The majority perpetrated against Latinos, Native Americans, and Asian Americans; more Latinos were lynched in*

California than were persons of any other race or ethnicity." (www.dukeupress.edu/books.php3?isbn=978-0-8223-3794-2   dnld: 11-25-07)

Alabama's Tuskegee Institute maintained statistics on lynching in America from 1882 - 1968. Their total: 4,749. Lynching peaked in the U.S. in the 1890s but some of the most highly publicized lynching occurred in the 1930s - 1950s, coinciding with America's fascination with eugenics. Anti-lynching crusader Ida B. Wells-Barnett lobbied for decades to make lynching a federal crime. In 2005 the Senate formally apologized for *failing to act* on some 200 anti-lynching bills. The resolution states that the Senate *"expresses the deepest sympathies and most solemn regrets of the Senate to the descendants of victims of lynching, the ancestors of whom were deprived of life, human dignity and the Constitutional protections accorded all citizens of the United States."*

Within populations with such aberrant treatment and conditions in common, a pattern emerges, one that churns out large numbers of self-destructive youth over generations seemingly from nowhere and everywhere. And, as began with the US Cavalry generations earlier, we simply continue to declare war on them rather than attempt to understand and then ameliorate the processes that result in such violence.

Not all groups that evolved gangs were subjected to such terrorism. And for some groups such as Poles, Irish, Jews and Italians, a point was reached where community violence retreated. One must study their entire dynamic, their social histories for how, why and under what conditions some became violent and it ended while others remain violent.

Broaden the search to find answers

Determining which groups were and are subjected to the worst treatment in America is not the point. Determining relationship with kinds, levels and durations of community violence *is* the point, regardless of group and location.

The current method for treating gangs and violence involve science in that solutions follow what are referred to as "best practices" also directed at *outcomes*. What would science reveal about historical violence perpetrated against groups that evolved "reservation communities" as an *outcome*? And processes of multi-generational trauma, dehumanization and marginalization? And conduct in-depth relational studies of the full effects of racism, slavery, lynching, murder, rape, and… until the process is arrested and treated and finally ended. Damage is still being perpetrated on next generations.

How can science help us to understand the violent reactions beyond "peers and bad parents" or the "turf, status and revenge" paradigm? Can we move beyond a biased search for a "warrior gene", and the assumption of an inherited, cultural or probable "genetic predisposition to violence" from Aztec and Zulu Warrior ancestors as fundamental bases for gangs? The objective should be to deconstruct the entire violence and peace dynamic from **outcome** to source and back again. We certainly have the means if we can find the will. Proper research *can* test correlations between self-destructive behaviors and the types, duration and severity of shared traumas among affected groups over generations…past, present - and *future*.

Part 2

Life on the "reservation"

...they exist in an upside-down world where perversions of love, power, honor and respect are there to bask in until it is their turn to die...

8

The Rise of the Urban Soldier…
…and failure of civil rights

*Even as youth continue to form into violent groups, a larger question is
one that has been of prime concern in minority communities for decades:
How did it come about that their youth could believe it necessary to act
out against each other in such deadly fashion?*

No one inherits a predisposition to kill or a desire to die bravely for a
gang name. Young people are not natural born killers, raised and bred to
form groups that only exist to murder each other. As earlier stated, the
process goes *from the outside in,* affecting the collective psyche of each
new generation long before such impact becomes manifest. Our culture
and institutions affect learning and subsequent behavior of children by
group. Lessons are positive for some and negative for others and deeply
ingrained in American thought and action. *Whether a young person decides
to join a gang or go to college is a logical consequence of purposeful learning
and socialization.*

In America, ethnic and racial minority groups have developed coping
mechanisms for survival *at home* even as we enlisted in worldwide life and
death struggles against hate, intolerance and persecution.

We continue to represent this country in all areas of social, economic and political arenas, winning gold medals, Nobel's and Pulitzers, inventing gadgets, running companies; building highways, skyscrapers, homes and railroads; fighting fires, washing cars, cleaning windows, healing the sick and raising our children. But we labor under a love-hate relationship that places us back on "reservations" at the end of the day.

Saluting our flag and proudly wearing the love of this country mattered little. Positive accomplishments remained largely hidden from view while negative caricatures were plentiful. History ignored our many achievements and media used us for villain fodder and cheap laughs. Groups remain under attack and are thus diminished in everyone's eyes, but especially in the eyes of children starving for heroes and a place in this country besides gangs, prisons and graveyards.

The demeaning of a people has been so commonplace we often miss it or minimize its impact. And most have learned to swallow hard but keep trying. *But once upon a time in each group's history, the societal violence became too much to bear, the shoddy education too blatant to dismiss, the jobs became too much to lose and laws, written and unwritten, too uneven to follow.*

At certain points, members of each group reacted. As was inevitable, irresistible forces met immovable objects and everything changed forever. While each targeted community struggled to live and let live, a dual activist response began to take shape regardless of "reservation" or geography. One response was armed with truth and justice; the other response was just armed.

The first to respond were those who took up the mantle of civil and human rights, wanting to stop the unbridled and rampant hatred and violence and the social injustice connected to it, and to raise the wounded child's level of self-love and pride in heritage, history and culture that had suffered for decades. There emerged armies of civil rights warriors of all colors, faiths and walks.

They are the activists marchers, Freedom Riders, farm workers, youth counselors, political party and community organizers and the rebel educators promoting African-American pride, Raza Movimientos and Native American emergence; and writers, attorneys, students, moms and dads that, sometimes on shaking ground, stood then and still stand up to armed forces, governors, mayors, and even friends and neighbors over basic human rights and dignity for all Americans. They dug in, fought back and fought hard in a struggle for decency, respect and honest treatment. Many were prosecuted, some murdered. They were labeled radicals, militants, communists, rabble-rousers, anarchists and… a threat to America. And a compliant media carried these messages forth. They and their families were trampled under horse's hooves, jailed and murdered for refusing to knuckle under, or to stand idly by and let the rights go and the blood flow.

They were and are America's unsung heroes. These modern pioneers represent every group never wanting to see another human being suffer even one more injustice due to their belonging to the wrong group in the wrong place at the wrong time. Activists still struggle to save futures and to save America from further division, warfare and embarrassment in the eyes of the world and in the eyes of God. Their numbers seem fewer now and the lines blurred but the work still goes on.

However, even as these warriors engaged in battles over the Constitution and the Bill of Rights, battlegrounds of another type emerged in a new war that was lost from the very first casualty. This war was being waged on the very streets activists were seeking to save, and these good persons were at a loss to stop it. Youthful casualties were becoming increasingly evident, *but by their own hand.*

This next phase was inevitable: the rise of the contemporary urban soldier. These were also activists, but of a different cloth. They initially believed leaders who asked them to enlist in a new revolution, one that would fight peacefully for justice and for an end to inequality and discrimination.

They witnessed the trouncing, beating, jailing and slaughter of citizens who united, organized and marched for equal justice, equal opportunity and fair play. Youth were still left wondering how they would fit in a nation not meant for them, and some concluded that they did not. Societal separation by group was all but cemented, especially in the mind. And for generations that followed, adults and their children from toddlers to teens continued to be bombarded in all aspects of daily life: at work and play, on TV and in movies, in stories and lore, in hiring, promotions and in school and in lessons. And even while fighting this nation's wars, they got the message often and loud as to who the real Americans were and to them especially, who they were not. Some would learn to take society's rejection as displeasure at their ever being born.

Increasing numbers of non-white Americans began to accept society's rejection, determining that they were somehow unfit, unworthy and indeed, un-American; that they deserved nothing more than the contemptuous treatment their groups were being subjected to. To them the struggle was useless and to fight no longer necessary. Theirs was a desperate but hopeless response to the indignities of a sub-class existence. And once again, the anger floor was raised for next generations to inherit - and a new crucible was forged.

As the unrelenting bombardment continued, it had a destabilizing effect that would facilitate communities passing a critical tipping point. And many did the unexpected: *under the heavy burden of oppression and rejection, they caved in on themselves.* And true to typical dysfunctional family form, the "black sheep" emerged, took on the blame and acted out in self-destructive behavior, mixing uncontainable rage with a growing dislike and rejection of self and those like him. The seeds of violence planted and nourished over generations were beginning to bear fruit. These "black sheep" began to act out the anger and frustration of the community household in a classic form of misdirected rage. Even as others continued to brave the overwhelming elements in acts of civil disobedience, still hoping for a civilized solution, the "black sheep"

82

eventually took it to streets and alleys. They were no longer hoping for a civilized solution that to them no longer mattered. They took on a new role in a classic American play acted out in theaters of war throughout the country. *For what was never imagined was that the targeted populations would so internalize the loathing and ill will of the dominant society that they would actually incorporate their own demise into their way of life and social structure.*

As each new generation is confronted with the realities of hatred, prejudice and discrimination and all that these mean, some ingest the toxins. They become hopeless and disconnect from dreams earlier promised without finding a way to fulfill them. Instead they *engaged a socially modified method to raise collective value through artificial means using deviant stand-ins to fit abnormal conditions. They formed sub-economies, modified their logic and behaviors and began to engage in sadistic and masochistic acts to fit their created reality.*

These youth took on the task of completing society's desire to control, subjugate and eliminate. They began to do exactly the same things to each other as society does to their racial and ethnic groups. They employed their own final solution for society's problem children and did the unthinkable: they engaged in sociopath ethnic cleansing and began to kill each other off.

This form of youth violence is learned genocide: adopted self-hatred and self-loathing sufficient to destroy one's mirror image on sight, and feeling righteous in the process; making excuses and reasons without logic beyond that which helps accomplish the task of elimination. *These are programmed acts of genocide, but by one's own hand.*

And thus the seeds of modern gang violence were sown. Although no one knew it at the time, the first players began to graduate from bats and chains to knives and guns. The next soldiers would carry on. Their true parents were racism and prejudice that bore children who eventually hated themselves to death.

This lemming-like lifestyle belies their preset existence as society's fodder and prey. They become predator and prey on each other, programmed to an empty existence in jails, prison camps and graveyards.

Their gang activity is no less than civil upheaval: rioting, as they know how to riot. In the meantime, and through the same institutional machinations, the rest of society is programmed not only to accept it, but to help it along and even profit from it. They benefit by dereliction and default. It's all the same program and received as meant. We program the population with ideas of hate and disrespect for themselves and each other *by groups*. Our children then go out and execute the program.

Dehumanization and the mechanisms employed to achieve it are powerful and destructive forces especially when used en masse. After a time, combined forces, both overt and subtle, can crush the spirit of a people beginning with the most vulnerable.

One subtle example of how mainstream this has become is *Newsweek's* Education Program. In 1998, *Newsweek* began distributing their World Migration Map and education guide to elementary classrooms throughout the nation. The map shows migration within the various continents labeled Asia, Europe, etc. The United States is labeled "Anglo-America". Besides being historically misleading, this label sends a subtle but clear message to *all* children, Anglo and non-Anglo, still figuring out their place and future in this great country. The wars against indigenous cultures still rage as a result. Imagine being told after thousands of years of your people's existence that your ancestral homeland is no longer your homeland. The Newsweek map attempts to make such an argument acceptable. Each group receives the message as intended: one as a support to continued racist behavior and the other as a message of where in America you fit - and don't fit.

9

Enter the Soldiers

The Community Violence Dynamic:

Youth gang members romantically view themselves as the defenders of their territory, their people and/or their way of life, much as a citizen militia. Such meritorious action should be rewarded if actually true. Their distorted aim is to defend against and exact revenge upon their perceived enemies, whoever and wherever they may be, even if they must be created.

In so doing, they support the popular view that youth gangs are insatiable killers engaged in an endless cycle of murder and revenge. Sort of a Hatfield and McCoy and Old Testament justice rolled into urban America under the official heading, *cycle of violence.*

If you inquire of a gang member why he murders, maims, robs and rapes, primarily his own people, he will respond with seemingly nonsensical reasons and rationale relating to *turf, status and revenge.* We in all our wisdom accept his explanations as gospel. These responses get us nowhere in understanding the true nature except to add fuel to that rationale. They certainly fall short of providing a legitimate reason to do harm up to and including eliminating another person forever.

He may relate his actions to his gang's having "power". Here at least there is a relationship drawn between the powerlessness of a people and the power-seeking gang member. However, his actions are without logical direction or purpose. In this pursuit, he seeks power from the powerless. Frankly, he is confused and does not know why he does what he does. In actuality, he is reacting to stimuli much greater than any gang.

The idea of a Gang Leader is myth. No person can lead a group if no one is already primed to move in that direction. Gangs are not "lead" to mayhem. New leaders do not emerge to *lead* new generations to murder and riot. In "reservation communities" negative emotions are *never* far from exploding into violence – individually and collectively. Cumulative negative actions can result in negative reactionary behaviors.

Although empirically it would appear that the connection of destructive youth to a particular minority group would be obvious, such is not the case.

Causative aspects are *external to the group*. The true *gang infrastructure* is not within the gang itself or the gang community, but is more directly related to externally generated acts, their duration and severity *and the resulting processes* or cycle(s) *then* initiated within the affected community.

When sufficient numbers of a group suffer insult, the stage is set for the emergence of group reactive behavior.

Such a degree of insults can only emanate from a host society.

A people, having in-common real and/or perceived collective suffering can be pushed over the edge. It is a universal response.

Political and anti-war demonstrations are examples as are civil rights marches, worker actions and student walkouts. So are major uprisings.

Similar groups in different locations that experience parallel levels, types and durations of negative treatment can reach the same critical mass and violence tipping points at about the same time.

As mentioned earlier, the Boston Tea Party was triggered by negative societal treatment against their larger group, the Colonists. This was a particularly difficult relationship that turned out not to be possible. The intolerable and oppressive treatment eventually reached a high enough scale to begin a collective violent reaction that became The Revolutionary War.

There are steps in and steps out of *violence status*, just as there is for *peace status*. A once violent area can turn peaceful and vice-versa. The violence progression follows a sustained period of negative acts, policies and behaviors emanating from a host society. The peaceful community has experienced the opposite from that same society.

➤ The community violence dynamic is a progressive multi-level reactive process initiated by negative external stimuli.

➤ The levels of reaction generally reflect the degree or intensity of stress build-up in a community at critical points and the graduated mechanisms employed to obtain release when no other relief is available or sufficient.

➤ The violence reactive process manifests within a range of intensities that logically reflect common experience regardless of location. The most intense reaction is all-out rioting.

➤ Similar violent incidents may be triggered by similar events and circumstances in disparate locations having similar experience.

In times past, the riot level of violence would transpire in separate and distinct locations without necessarily disturbing other areas. However, since the advent of mass communication, it is possible to trigger riots in several locations by a single event such as happened in the so-called Rodney King riots. The verdict released anger that had built to explosive levels among similar groups although in different locations.

➤ Some groups may integrate cultural, religious and/or social factors into their reaction and response.

Though unseen or acknowledged as such, the same triggering dynamic is often at work among varied groups but with reactions filtered through particular cultural, religious and/or social mores. Their form of "rioting" or unrest and upheaval may therefore express itself in different ways and with slightly varying justifications.

Reactive community violence has occurred in parts of the Middle East. In some instances religion and culture influenced violent responses as unlikely men and women gave up their lives to express group outrage. In other situations, one nation's revolt triggered others suffering under common kinds and levels of oppression. Multiple groups in various locations were primed and ready to erupt pending the right triggering/facilitating event. It is therefore important to not dismiss the reaction as unrelated to the same kinds of negative forces.

➤ Incidents of community violence are final stage responses to longstanding negative stimuli. As levels of community stresses intensify, various processes, devices and vessels are progressively required to obtain sufficient release. The stresses are highest where the need is greatest. Once a tipping point is reached, the host society must exert extreme measures to rectify the now upended balance.

Outcomes at this stage are fatal. Once significant societal aspects turn sufficiently negative and the violence reactive process tipping point is breached, a negative and destructive progression is in place, regardless of group or location.

Violent groups and gangs may evolve in several areas among the same or similar groups with no connection to each other *except having experienced the same social history with the same host society.* This point was confirmed in the referenced 1992 study by Maxon, et al. showing gang onset had little or nothing to do with gang migration.

Communities that have in common type, level and duration of negative interactions and experiences manifest reactive violence patterns similarly within a range of intensities for that society. It is unlikely that a person will set themselves on fire in the town square in Buffalo, New York. Likewise, a riot will not likely occur among a group new to experiencing negative interactions and events. A meeting with their local representatives would be more in keeping. But a group that has experienced a range of traumatic experiences is likely to react in a progressively violent fashion reflecting their *social history*. As grievances accumulate, frustration, anger and resentment can build to explosive levels. Reactions may range from breaking a window, bullying a spouse or peer, screaming at an authority figure, to joining with others to collectively vent (gangs) and even participate in riotous rampage. The *range* will more or less reflect cumulative shared experience integrated with group mores and triggered at collective tipping points. The process is supported by underlying societal factors.

During the last 100 years, African-Americans have crossed the threshold to fiery rioting on several occasions. At the same time, other groups were at their own critical mass points crossing particular intensity thresholds. However, all groups that exhibit elevated and extreme levels of violence have reached a higher relative level of static anger regardless of time or place. He is angry and full of rage. The triggering and response levers are set and ready.

It is important to know that the affected community is wrought with confusion, bewilderment and denial at the *unjustified* negative acts directed at their group, even as they accept responsibility for the forms of violence that members of their group engage in.

What comes around - goes around...

Resentment, anger and rage develop within an affected group over generations in an *external-to-internal* dynamic... then travel back out again. The group experience results in relatively large numbers of disaffected youth within a concentrated area, the "reservation community".

A group is better able to absorb anger, rage, disappointment, sadness, grief, etc. than is an individual. A group can function as a release "spigot" if you will composed of those with the most battered and imperiled psyches. *It is at this stage that individual and/or family circumstances may place him as more or less likely to engage in collective anti-social behaviors per so-called risk and protective factors. He is primed for the release "triggering" stratagem stage under the "turf, status and revenge" paradigm. The client is reacting to* **outcomes.**

Early stage releases are inward-directed and may include substance abuse, family strife and serious thoughts of suicide. These initial stages reflect a childlike acceptance of blame for the group's status and condition. They may also indicate depression, hopelessness, despondency and elements of PTSD. As cumulative negative pressures require more release than just those aimed at self and at those closest, release activities eventually move outward and beyond the immediate family and out to a primed community. Negative forces reach a point where he and others in the community are ready to be "triggered" into negative group reactionary behavior - *the reactive internal-to-external response.* These can range from verbal and physical abuse and bullying to fisticuffs and other peer violence and then group warfare. Eventually they can and do proceed to all out rioting.

When riots do occur, the explosive release reduces stress levels to previous *inward-directed* violence. This is still community unrest, but at lower levels. The area then resumes counting victims as before the conflagration: "Gang killings are down eight percent over last year, from 87 to 80". And the phrase, "We have to give up on this generation and concentrate on the next" also resumes. So do "prevention" efforts. In current "Best Practices", the domains targeted involve the child and parent and ignores basic structural issues and social history.

In another country the entire reactive process may well have been reduced to acts of civil terrorism where institutions are primary targets and human tolls are mounted to make a point. *The lack of such terrorist response here confirms belief in this system and determination to work toward inclusion and acceptance...and that will never change no matter how harsh the conditions.* However, until such time that inclusion and acceptance overrides bias and exclusion, negative pressure will continue to be released in violent form…and as long as each affected group internalizes blame and responsibility for such turmoil, violence will remain primarily inward-directed with occasional outward explosions.

Violence is not accepted as normal. Violence is involuntary and even resisted. That chronic violence remains in a community over generations is indicative of serious long-term damage to the collective psyche sufficient to initiate and sustain self-destructive expressways to supposed release. But there is no release, only false beliefs and futile efforts in the vain hope of obtaining relief.

Obscuring honest and productive discussion that would lead to greater understanding is the mantra that society bears no blame, that there is something inherently wrong from within. This is like a sick person accepting blame for his illness. This self-blame aspect has been programmed in and is part and parcel of repeated critical mass build-up and violence release modalities for groups of youthful reactionaries – the so-called *cycle of violence.*

10

The Community Family Under Pressure

Youth gang violence is a phenomenon seemingly linked to the primary causes of turf, status and revenge. In actuality, it is one aspect of a set of responses to negative societal interaction and stimuli in common with the same and other groups of similar circumstance, history and status.

Dehumanization and marginalization are atypical to majority members of society but typical in "reservation communities". As these are abnormal forces, so there are abnormal reactions.

As noted, artificial reasons are *created* to accommodate the extraordinary need for reaction and release, e.g. 'colors' and 'turf', which are so common they can easily expand to accommodate an elevated rage release need among a large population simply by separating along *more colors, more streets, more landmarks, ad infinitum.* The entire process can become cyclic and include other violence formats.

Rodney King was not the *cause* of the 1992 riots, but merely a *trigger* to release a large amount of built-up community pressure that existed in various parts of the country among the same group at about the same time.

The televised beating was felt hard in all "reservation communities" already immersed in constant stages of imploding. Non African-American "reservation" dwellers knew the lid was about to be blown off for their fellow Americans. Even as their own communities were experiencing lower levels of unrest and upheaval, their fellow black reservation communities had been **imploding** at maximum stages (gang wars) and were again bordering on **explosion** in a repeat of the final stages of the *societal cycle of violence* – RIOTS. The last apex being during the 1960's. The Rodney King beating put groups in-sync although unaware of the other's readiness. The subsequent courthouse acquittal triggered what was primed to occur. However, without such a "triggering" event the community is successfully contained and the process remains internal within the aggrieved community.

Again consider the Colonists and even experiences in the Middle East. Entire groups were primed and ready to react, some violently. When the tipping point was finally breached, they exploded in upheaval per the time and place and social considerations. In some cases there are religious and in others secular influences. These are examples of an oppressed citizenry finally pushed to rise up. They may include students and young people, doctors, lawyers, housewives and househusbands – the community. The principle is the same as is the outcome.

Gangs to riots

We wonder rhetorically what could possible bring an adolescent to the point of becoming ready to kill and be killed by other young people. Thus the conclusions are reached that he or she must have inherited a genetic predisposition to violence and/or "gets it" from his friends, family and culture. Or simply, "it's in their blood".

A young mind must go through stages before reaching a level of killer-readiness. Here a child becomes gang-ready first then learns to be trigger-ready later.

The process to gang readiness has an *origin* that usually involves violent introduction of his group to a society followed by pejorative *social conditioning* mainly through institutions, and eventual aberrant

adaptation to his hostile environment. Once achieved, he is a vessel at the ready for violent activity.

He is usually a child from a community where many now suffer from chronic symptoms of clinical depression such as difficulty sleeping, fatigue, feelings of hopelessness and worthlessness, self-hate and inappropriate guilt, difficulty concentrating, agitation, social isolation, feelings of being helpless to change it and thoughts of death and suicide.

Indeed, a survey of inner-city students in Los Angeles, Ca. revealed many were suffering from various forms of clinical depression. (http://articles.latimes.com/2008/apr/26/local/me-survey26**).** They also exhibited repressed anger. It is this environment (social ecology) where youth emerge that are "trigger-ready" for implosion and eventual explosion. These *outcomes* of negative social conditioning and environmental adaptation combine with oftentimes negative aspects within his home and family life.

This violent child has formed a maximum, negative self-image and is full to overflowing of anger and rage. He is at the fringe of his community (black sheep) acting out the rage and frustration profoundly felt by the community "family". He has engaged in a desperate search for release and hooks up with others seeking the same release. Gang youth are anger-based although the bases for such anger are not understood. He directs his anger at those he blames most for his situation and thus hates deeply and will do maximum harm to, on sight, with minimal provocation – *his mirror image.*

Anger is not able to be contained, nor is it limited to him and his cohorts but is generalized community anger that over generations has breached critical mass and tipping point stages. Groups with elevated levels of violence have greater numbers of individuals looking for an immediate release of pent-up anger - *they need to explode.*

What *is* usable from the government's entire ethnic street gang analysis is the final stage of violence readiness, the triggering stratagem stage. This final stage produces dead bodies presumably over issues of *turf, status and revenge.* What is missed is that these three aspects are merely "triggers" to violence and not *causes* of violence.

Non-ethnic violent youth (white) may also finally explode over *what appear* to be issues of *turf, status and revenge,* but as seen *from their own perspective and limited negative experience.* They adopt what they perceive to be a traditional gang model, but with their own variations sufficient to differentiate friend from foe in order to identify an "enemy" to explode on. Their violence is labeled differently however even though engaging in the same kinds of activities. Their behaviors are less onerous and their issues solvable – even when they shoot up a school.

As example, the Columbine incident will never be referred to as a gang shooting involving *turf, status or revenge,* although under the current gang violence paradigm, these would suffice to classify the incident as a gang shooting as *status* and *revenge* were clearly involved as "triggers". In this instance however, causal relationships were and continue to be well researched without regard to gang motives. The *causes* of the Columbine massacre were looked at sans the triggering stratagem stage and treated as an anomaly but one that *can* be understood and therefore mitigated. Steps to do so were immediate and comprehensive *for that group. As a result, the opportunity to learn valuable lessons of how violence can emerge among a broader universe of disaffected youth are lost.* The killing of the Columbine children was maintained as "different" from the beginning. But was it?

We see gang formations among many groups: male and female, Bloods and Crips, barrio warriors, tribal warriors, white power Nazis, rebels, stoners, skinheads, cycle gangs, gays and straight, surfers, skateboarders and bicycle riders. We see them among immigrants as well as homegrown, ethnic and non-ethnic, by culture and race, geography and ideology - all out to protect their group or defend a "territory."

Youth gang formation and subsequent activities are a generic response by youth from groups that are, or believe they are becoming marginalized as a group, family, community or a people.

This social response is no longer limited to racial and ethnic minorities.

It is a force that can emerge anywhere and anytime, including those newly marginalized or fear they may be. While members of some groups believe it their duty or fate to join a gang, others default into it by believing that they are at the margins of society, or that group "pecking-order" will change at their expense and they seek protection via a countering force. It is indeed telling that any group should *fear* being a minority group in this country. This fear may be reason to form protective gangs, or ersatz citizen militias. Gangs rise up as soldiers out of desert sand, ready to defend their group from "alien" **forces**.

11

One Nation, Under God....

Each week in America about 18 people are erased forever by gang violence. Someone's son, daughter, mother or father had a past, present and future until a few moments ago and another is getting ready to die...each time of death frozen forever in the hearts of loved ones. By definitions and explanations we have ignored external social forces affecting violence among young people, instead seeing the color of gangs and blaming that. There is too much evidence slamming our sensibilities to dismiss this phenomenon as a minority problem that only touches kids from the other side of the tracks. The tracks have disappeared.

Something is changing. Some groups are wising up and others are getting caught in the whirlpool. However one looks at it, the shift is on and the machinery is straining to adjust. Something is changing right before us, but we don't see it until the explosions rip our hearts out. Violent and enraged youth is still the prolific by-product; haters of other youth plain and simple, but always, why?

Growing up in America can be a hazardous experience. Children are being sideswiped as they try to live and let live. Friends are getting hurt and hurt bad and their other friends are doing it. For growing numbers of America's children, missing one's childhood is tough luck; to witness a crime a rite of passage; to be a victim means you weren't paying attention.

Anywhere can be the wrong place and anytime can be the wrong time. Angry encounters can in a blinding flash become deadly. Merely taking a walk or making a verbal misstep can have lethal repercussions. The end may be just around the corner, down the street, at a party or on the schoolyard.

Youth are learning that they better get tough or get out of the way. Parents see their children dressing down for the occasion instead of dressing up for their futures. Young people know the new playground rules. It's tough luck if they don't like them.

This reality has been the standard in traditional gang areas for generations, but explained and accepted as something intrinsic to a people. But violence has hit home where we never expected.

Why do young people feel a need to "do in" other youth? What is it about a society that pits one child against another to the death? This is not one nation vs. another, this is a nation that stands together one nation, under God, as the epitome of democracy. Why are we known as much for our gangs as we are for our freedoms? What is affecting our youth this way? Even new arrivals seem to know the rules and how to play. But just what game is this? We state high ideals and fairness and strive to maintain a national moral compass. Do we follow that compass?

King of the mountain?

The United States of America *is* different and the differences cut both ways. We set out to be a nation of freedoms and equal opportunity and uniquely guided by a higher power that sees man in His image. This is not to begin a religious argument but merely to state the obvious...*In God We Trust*. As a democracy, we believe in freedom for all. That anyone can succeed. Here is another way of looking at it:

America can be looked at as a highly competitive place, even predatory. Competition is fierce and any advantage is a fair one. Survival and success is often at the expense of others. In the grand social scheme, youth may be players in a contest that we as a society have put in place.

Youth may be following a pattern of categorizing themselves and others into a hierarchal subsystem of groups relating to social positioning in an ongoing quest for *power* - getting it, adding to it, holding onto it and passing it down. Some get pummeled in a burgeoning struggle over social and economic one-upmanship.

The Founding Fathers set wheels in motion by adopting a caste system to empower their personal wealth. They adopted national rules of conduct contained in the Constitution and the Bill of Rights intended however, for European white males. Even their mothers, sisters and daughters were excluded from the array of freedoms as originally outlined. As a result, America's pledges of freedom, democracy, equal rights and opportunity have not yet been delivered on as promised.

From our humble beginnings, we struggle with one and both. That is, the Founding Fathers had in mind a new world that broke from all tradition and what was seen as a failing in other empires. E.g., slavery and all that came with it were detested and argued against by some. But where one stands depends on where one sits. Ultimately, lofty words were used as guide toward that new world, but then as today, how these are interpreted are the bases of what we as a nation struggle with.

The American Dream is caught in a Utopian conundrum: How does a nation deliver on its stated guarantees of freedom and equality to all when it was meant for the benefit of a few? From our nation's beginning and to this day, this dilemma persists. And we as a nation struggle to assure that justice is indeed for all and that rules are applied evenly.

How can some profess to be part of one nation under an all-loving God and hate some of his children? Our history reveals a conflicting social history to say the least. How does our social history relate to "reservation community" violence dynamics?

Power as power… good and bad

The quest for success rides on the quest for power. To attain power both the caste system and the promise of freedoms are operating in one social system. With each decade we see evidence of groups succeeding while others watch and dream. No bells go off we just know a new group has "made it". Women, gays and some nationalities have found their "power ladder" in the American scheme of things. And it is also obvious which groups have not.

The "reservation community" gang member does not have a clue as to how or why his people became inert. He does not consider that his group is a cog in a larger machine. That they are engaged in the same quest for power as any other group. That those who have power will use it to keep it that way. He does not consider that his forebears had to fight against overwhelming odds for every bit of access to resources, to "overcome adversity" in every aspect of daily life. And why he is always so angry.

He takes the game to the street where a mutated version of "power" is attainable. And we have decided to leave it at that. Yet he will never stop being an American. You will not see "reservation" terrorist groups against this country even as their youth destroy themselves and each other. You *will* continue to see people of color fight and die in our nation's wars to protect all of our freedoms. You will also see their veterans come back to a society that does little to help their group achieve their American Dream.

Power is selfishly held. Its evidence is all around "reservation communities"… its militaristic side all too visible. Powerful decisions are made somewhere by someone unseen and without fanfare. Power…and the ability to have it, maintain it, to grow it and to use it must be shared. For without sharing the bountiful side of what power can bring, we guarantee a social system that derails collective progress and an unbalanced status-quo. And this "power war" is a drain on all Americans.

Your gang?

Some may view the American Dream as not meant to be shared…as a zero-sum game - that for one to succeed another must lose. They may perceive that should members of some groups move up in economic and social stature, theirs would necessarily move down, that their group would be in danger of becoming marginalized.

Family disruption and economic deterioration is spreading as more find it difficult going to hold on to their power and the gap between rich and poor widens. In America money represents power as power trades in money. As families under economic stress join, or fear joining, the foreign ranks of the lower classes, they feel increasingly threatened. Some may fear their children will experience the dark world of street survival that all know is lurking. Some are already there. As these youths values adjust to those previously observed from a safer distance, they choose their allies and enemies from a growing list of players also seeking power and strength through numbers. They latch on to seemingly proven methods of the street survivalist's world, thinking they'll come out whole on the other end but miscalculate the costs of their involvement. This second world is not where many would choose to be.

Such fears and insecurity bolster rules of separation and favoritism. Some try to ensure the "wrong" people do not fall into this chasm not meant for them. Children get with the program and join ongoing and well-established contests of group exclusion and one-upmanship. They qualify and quantify groups and learn to place them in a social and economic pecking order. Next generations of employers, teachers, CEO's and political leaders carry these beliefs to their institutional placement. They act to preserve a traditional social alignment be it lending at a bank, teaching in a school or serving on a jury. They may be members of congress or the local service club. In this way, some are guided to success and others off a cliff.

The process leading to such social violence cannot be traced and is impossible to track as it resides in the belief structure of a people. It justifies social and economic acts, policies and behaviors against peoples based on differences…and power. It inhibits friendly interaction and instead reinforces longstanding "natural enemies" lists. Negative belief is a prime factor as it sets up and reinforces institutional rage build-up, group conflict and societal disharmony.

A necessary evil?

For this discussion, accept the following for a moment:

- Groups have been conquered and enslaved to build a nation that espouses freedoms, equal opportunity and fairness but that only benefits certain segments of the population;

- anger, resentment and violent reaction among those used up in the process are logical consequences; and

- gangs and community violence have evolved in reaction to the preferential economic and social system, ergo

- Gang's existence is a cost of doing America's business and as such, a necessary evil.

If this were not so, would we remain so easily confused over the process and remain deaf, dumb and blind over the tens of thousands of our children's violent deaths? If this were not so, wouldn't we do whatever it takes to find the true roots of this youth elimination program? If this were not so, would we resist efforts to end exclusion and preferential treatment as possible links to such violent outcomes?

Gangs form among groups that have the same negative societal positioning in common, even though having nothing in common related to their cultures, upbringing or genetic pool. There are winners and there are losers in the larger game. Survival of the fittest is the mantra. Those with the fewest supports fall first, disposable as so much fodder. Those with the fewest supports are by design, concentrated in "reservation communities" where the power game is deadly.

In spite of such daunting odds and adversity, individuals and eventually groups do fight their way into the social mainstream. As each group becomes increasingly included their rage dissipates but usually followed by another group that takes its former place, receiving the wrath of dehumanization in turn. For this is the system we have. This manner of "competition" extends from the highest levels of business and government to the streets where we see the results as youth violence.

A Dream not yet fulfilled

As each new group arrives to this land of natives, immigrants and slaves, they find easy going or difficult going depending on color, nationality, origin, religion and circumstances. As time goes on and some experience successful integration, difficulties reduce as does the rage and conflict. We saw this with Irish, Poles, Jews and others. We have yet to see it with those still locked into "reservation communities", natives, slaves and some others.

America is really no different than any other nation in history except in its precepts, but it is these precepts that make all the difference. The American promise of equal opportunity, justice and democracy is the light of Freedom for the world. It is this American promise that we have struggled with from the beginning.

Gangs were not here when this country was founded, although groups that are now active were. But gangs were not a part of their reality. At some point gang violence came into being and has expanded exponentially within this society and in similar societies. So where are we? How far have we come? How much further do we Americans need to go?

12

War, what is it good for?

Throughout history extraordinary efforts have been made to avoid conflicts and find peaceful solutions wherever and whenever possible, the sanctity of life being the overriding concern. However, conflict can occur over governance or when resources are at stake. Conflict is sometimes necessary for social change. Some of our social bastions are indefensible but will not topple until the full connection is made between our brand of civil conflict and social inequities.

We had quietly declared an enemy and then we publicly declared war.

The accepted explanations for relative high numbers of violent minority youth are remarkably similar even though groups are separated by geography, ethnicity, culture and other fundamentals. The relationship between a society's negative social history with a group and that group's youth violence has not been factored in. We have simply concluded that there are high numbers of killer-youth among certain definable groups that murder one another for no apparent reason save for *turf, status and revenge,* and can only be stopped by armed force and imprisonment. Hence the "War on Gangs" has become part of the American lexicon.

War is a result of failed social, economic and political policies as they affect a populace.

War is declared in situations that do not respond to peaceful efforts and solutions. It is politics by other means. War is targeted, purposeful all-out destruction of an enemy. War should always be the theater of last resort. In this case, we have opted to embrace a military war posture, even though the best stance is to never go to war in the first place.

Political, social, economic and corporeal war had long been declared on sectors of the population, who then declared war on each other, and we declared war on the combatants - a true cycle of violence with no end.

Declaring war on groups already suffering under economic, political and social violence is *not* searching for peaceful and humane solutions. It is exacerbating conditions that sustain conflict and *creates more recruits*. To continue the warlike posture is folly as it has no (positive) end game.

An analogy is trying to win WWII by killing and imprisoning Nazi soldiers (violent gangs) then going after Hitler Youth seen hanging out together, wearing their Nazi uniforms (injunctions) at ever earlier ages (and their parents) but *ignoring Adolph, Mein Kampf, the German government, the economic and political culture and a complicit media that ushered in such behaviors in the first place.* If this had been the plan, we would still be fighting a losing battle there, too, all the while wondering why they just keep coming.

Gang violence is *our* war matrix extended to the civilian populace. This radical form of civil unrest and upheaval is a people's response to society's failed policies as regards particular groups.

Once war has been declared, the goal is to win by any and all means necessary. In the process we place the civil rights of entire communities at risk and use up financial resources that not only might bring the conflict to an end, but may have prevented war in the first place.

Cops and bangers engage in a synergistic dance of defiance as the rest of us hang on to empty promises of a military victory over a socially manufactured enemy.

In the absence of a coherent understanding of community violence processes, disagreement reigns. And whether over reasons for conflict, how best to fight the war, the fair use of resources or the political power that would direct such resources, peaceful discussions and solutions are on hold "until the land is secure" or until such time that peace becomes more beneficial than continued conflict. Under the current paradigm, this cannot occur.

Change can only occur if and when we see a benefit and adopt a strategy to connecting real causes with real solutions.

In the meantime the confusion persists in all areas involved with this war - which is all areas of society. Misdirection and confusion effectively trump true understanding and therefore peaceful discussion and therefore solutions and the beginning to an end of *this* war.

A war model leads to a system of analysis and actions that fits the war context: enemy logistics, war strategies and prisoner counts. This is where we remain stuck – a war between the gangs as stand-ins for devastated "reservation communities", and the armed forces, and society remains strangely detached through tens of thousands of deaths and hundreds of thousands of injuries, imprisonments and tattered and destroyed family and community fabric.

There is a definite societal process at work that grabs hold and places each child in jeopardy. And at each stage elements that usher in next stages. Once the process begins, a child is not left with a decision to join or not to join a gang. It is not that simple. He or she is making the best of the circumstances presented and had no say as to the acceptance or rejection of *the elements* that ushered in the warlike environment. He is instead left to make an artificial decision between society (good) and his family, peers, culture, history, heritage and genetic pool (bad).

At this stage his decision is at a deeper more profound level. It resides at the level of the *self* and the process of how an identity is constructed. This secondary part of the process is *inside-out* rather than *outside-in.* It is however, guided by external elements that should have no place in his decision-making process about who he is and where in the world he fits.

While warfare rages, the population is in increased danger as collateral damage occurs from both sides generating casualties by armed forces *as well as* the local combatants. Gangs target by appearance and some law enforcement officers have made the same judgments. Both may view some 'villagers' as unfriendly in the war environment, that they provide "support and sustenance" to the enemy. Gangs see a victim as legit as long as they reside in enemy territory. Thus the community truly resembles a battleground as casualties of the two wars mount: the "gang war" and the "War on Gangs".

The "War on Gangs" is not winnable by trying to identify combatants among civilians in a combat zone. Added firepower will not win a war where each soldier voluntarily marches to his own end and is immediately replaced due to systemic forces beyond the street gang milieu. These "soldiers" are created by social influences that simply do not respond to armies or imprisonment. The potential for devastation and human suffering has been and continues to be too great to be left to the armed combatants on all sides to solve. Calm and reason must prevail.

Males in "reservation communities" are systematically decimated mentally, emotionally and physically and are already 'missing in action'.

Even as they battle each other to their deaths, the criminal justice system cannot hope to contain the numbers generated from these aberrant circumstances. And taken to its logical end, if each of the over one million gang members were arrested today, the criminal justice system would collapse under the weight, *yet we continue in that direction.*

As currently pursued, the "War on Gangs" guarantees more conflict, massive imprisonment, more injuries and more deaths.

One consequence of attacking community violence militarily is to permanently set in place the mindset and the means to wage war and escalate as necessary. Information flow regarding violent youth continues to come primarily from those armed forces charged with solving it *and* those who would benefit. Their explanations describe war efforts, numbers and stratagem. Law enforcement now uses "terrorist" and "terrorist threats" as a legal devise against minority youth.

When will they ever learn?

Vietnam should have taught us that going to war requires an understanding of the dynamics of war beyond bombs and bullets, or run the very real risk of losing in the long run.

Vietnam was thought to be going well as long as the numbers were in our favor. We then learned that numbers can be manipulated and do not tell the entire story. Oftentimes the numbers game is merely that: a "body count" and "prisoner count" that lets us know how the war is "progressing". Vietnam also taught us that 'enemies' are not always as advertized. Propaganda is as much a part of a war effort as guns, bombs and fighter pilots. For public consumption, media provides glimpses into the gang world limited to the violent act and our response to such acts. Popular media exploits them in TV dramas and movies then covers the killing fields on the evening news. Historically, America's minorities have been profiled by popular media as violent criminals, or not at all.

War involves people in the worst ways and carries a heavy cost. War has no positive impact on underlying problems and ignores the people.

A "second world" is in place and we battle with its soldiers.

If you are going to start a war, you must have a strategy. The absence of a strategy invites chaos. We are left with a strategy of chaos, *which may indeed be the strategy.*

Chaos as logic…an overview from behind the scenes

Gangs and elevated levels of community violence release pent up anger, rage and resentment. Gangs fill some needs but with deviant replacement versions. These cross the line between civility and lawbreaking. Law enforcement and justice agencies are needed to deal with the results and resources must go there. However, evidence is overwhelming that classrooms, libraries, sports and recreation and other family-friendly infrastructure and resources are *not* budgeted to structurally *improve* "reservation communities". Federal, state and local funds have been and continue to be unevenly directed as a matter of course. Indeed, had educational, family and community friendly decisions been made evenly, the "reservation community" would not exist, nor would their death defying gangsters. Under the 'War on Gangs' as solution scenario, decisions to direct resources toward military and prisons are routinely made. In order to bring some order from the chaos, *some structural changes will have to be made.*

History is a record of beliefs turned to actions

The belief based actions that got us here are still in place so tomorrow's history will reflect what we, you and I, do to make corrections, or not do. If nothing changes today, nothing will change tomorrow...unless *you* decide to change it.

> *It will always cost more to house a prisoner than to give him/her an Ivy League education, but apparently worth every cent.*

The prison-industrial complex built up around various group's violent youth is appallingly expensive both in dollars and human costs. As in all wars, some profit from various aspects of war's tremendous expenditures. The humanity aspect is reduced or forgotten in times of war. We consider the numbers of dead and injured as enemies of our civilization and "getting what they deserve". All expenditures are allowed to vanquish our shared enemies. What we cannot see is that we created the enemy and the war.

Gangs are entrenched and growing wildly. The chaos around gangs and the efforts to suppress them are out of control. However, this place we find ourselves evolved from a seed, was nurtured and it blossomed. We have to dig up that seed rather than continue to simply clip its shoots. At the same time we must interrupt the "nurturing" process.

We have allowed the evolution of a system that fosters hopelessness and failure for generations of "reservation" youth. As the rest of society progresses with discoveries and opportunities the educational disparity alone effectively idles large numbers of otherwise productive young people. It would be infinitely more civilized to use the relatively few resources required to fix what is broken rather than the vast resources needed to monitor, lock up and hold our aberrant creations. We now lock up more minority males (potential fathers of intact families) for longer periods than any time in history. And the young women are catching up. It is past time to change our strategy. This "war" is **without logic or strategy to end it.**

In this war the machinery is clogged with minority youngsters – the hope and future of a people. Jails, prisons and graveyards are full of once colorful children somehow responsible for all this mayhem and seemingly out to bring down society.

The entire debacle is much more than any debilitated community could possibly dream up.

This "war" is not between superpowers or even heavily armed governments with an air force, army, navy or marines. This is a conflict whereby generations of large numbers of young people self-destruct in very personal ways. We are living at a time of our history where extraordinarily elevated numbers of young people from groups that have a shared history of being subjected to societal terror and annihilation are annihilating each other. This phenomenon begs serious research for a serious and humane solution. To not care if you live or die by age 12 is not a normal childhood or a good case for our civilization. This is all the result of a purposely mistaken identity of the true reasons for youth violence. Yet the proffered guise of an unstoppable *cycle of violence* remains strangely serviceable.

As time marches on and the "wars" continue, and youth continue to eliminate each other, young soldiers get stuck in the *effects* part of the *cause and effect scheme* and dead bodies mount. The origins of their group anger are lost or were never understood in the first place.

Youth who are angry at the world do not consider that their people are in a constant state of civil unrest and upheaval - as recipients and as perpetrators. Nor do they consider that the first "riots" were in the hearts and minds of their forebears who suffered from much more severe acts and attitudes against them as a people. The pain and anger accumulates with each generation then transfers to newborns the hopelessness, resentment and rage ready for triggering.

As youth gangs entrench and evolve, newer participants are further removed from their true cultural identity but also from gang predecessors. They are less forgiving and bereft of emotion. A lack of social feeling becomes pronounced with each new group. They are quick to react rather than reflect. The question of how and why the anger originated is far removed from the urge to act immediately and violently. If we don't get it, that's our problem. He knows enough about his world to die for it. We do not know the basics of his world nor his thinking. However, when conditions for a gang identity to be formed exist, all of our futures are less secure.

Although racial dynamics are constantly changing, the process remains intact. The faces and nomenclature may change but the beat goes on. Racial animosity is on the increase and will be the next big thing with Hybrids close behind. Lines will continue to be crossed.

As white youth forge into the homeboy world, their neighborhoods are less safe. These newest soldiers are coming from communities where this was not supposed to happen. Angry enough to do something or feeling pushed to participate in this all-American pastime, white youth struggle on the same slippery slope never intended to reach their homes or insulated learning centers. Some are bolstering their weakening spirits around skinhead movements and Gothic dances with the devil. Others are emulating the more established homeboy gangster movement, seeking the already invented and perfected wheel and rolling with it.

We are all in the same gang. However, even as false and simplistic reasoning and acceptance of ethnic youth violence persists, white players are being separated away with their anger and rage issues being addressed in a holistic manner. Their parents are not told that we must give up on their generation of babies and concentrate on the next. No one would dare and hope to keep their government job. To go part of the way with only some of our youth will not end this spreading nightmare.

As long as basic issues are not addressed, the gang-game will change even as it remains the same. It will continue to be deadly serious but with new and different players. Some will no longer aim only at each other's tribes. Almost every group has a militia that is armed and dangerous. This is another century, but still the continuation of our own modern day civil war.

13

The Cycle of Violence Fallacy
(if not a "war", what is it?)

The classic cycle of violence explanation for youth killing youth is described as an endless and reciprocal series of local battles to the death over turf, status, colors, graffiti and the consequent taking revenge for earlier killings. It limits the gang problem to issues of cultural idiosyncrasies, family upbringing and historical rivalries. Explaining it this way creates and reinforces a mindset in the society in which it operates which all parties come to accept: that some groups are by nature violent, malevolent and self-destructive. Such misdirection and misunderstanding hampers solution...

Some offer "solutions" that reflect their frustration and their bias, "put them all in a coliseum and let them kill each other off". They take the assumption of innate self-destructive behavior at face value. However, there is no historical evidence of such self-destructive behavior over such intangibles as colors, graffiti and non-owned land (turf) that continues without end in the history of *any* of the warring groups. That we accept a gang *cycle of violence* reflects a belief construct that goes against human history and traditional human behavior. Real wars are fought over real land, real resources and real power. There is an eventual end to the conflict based on some *tangible* objective being reached, or by negotiated settlement over those tangibles.

The gang war dynamic bears no relationship to "real" wars. There is no "objective" nor can there ever be. This war goes nowhere, has no logic and in all its destructive madness has no tangible benefit. Therefore, under this paradigm, *there is no possible end.* The only thing this war accomplishes is subjugation and elimination, a strategy learned and adopted over time and experience resulting from a series of catastrophic clashes of cultures and self-serving societal designs.

Gangs as armed forces are not organized to win wars, gain resources, change policies or topple regimes. They are an aberration unique to societies whose beliefs, traditions, policies and practices place entire groups at untenable disadvantage.

A social system cannot divorce itself from its parts. There is no "them and us". We are all part of a socio-ecosystem where each part is affected by the other. When one part is sick we all feel the symptoms, sooner or later.

Gangs *cannot* form or continue without presence of fundamental social abnormalities being a constant source of friction that only a host society can initiate, control and maintain.

The groups that evolved gangs here experienced some difficulty with European groups, e.g., African slaves; North American natives including some Latino groups; and some Asian and Pacific Islander groups. A clash of cultures would be an understatement. These introductions were fraught with conflict, unrest and upheaval. Our groups that evolved gangs experienced directed violence, marginalization, exploitation and dehumanization in their interactions with society as a matter of course. This combination would logically lead some to violent expression. Our gangs would not exist otherwise. And they could not keep going without such "support".

"Civilization" means evolving and advancing a society, *all* of a society. It means advancement, improvement and access and opportunity for all of its citizenry…and humanism. Otherwise, *it is not a civilization that can legitimately continue on a path of advancement.*

In the "war against gangs", military power and control over "reservation communities" continues the original path of containment, control and maintenance of groups as commodity. These similarly treated but geographically separate communities continue to lose ground while non-reservation communities enjoy increasingly supportive resources and the social advantages and advances as originally designed. The latter advances civilization while the former retards it. Eventually, it goes nowhere.

A "cycle of violence" can be ended anytime we wish to end it. We just have to *want* to end it.

14

The Cycle of Maintenance

Professionals generally agree that multi-generational patterns must be interrupted to stop a "cycle of violence". However, in reservation communities, all anti-violence efforts are after the fact - after the formation of a cycle(s)...and the subsequent declarations of "war".

Prevention programs as we know them *are not preventative* as they react to established **outcomes** of systemic processes.

A Community Violence Prevention Program must be comprehensive and aimed at source (origin), process (evolution) <u>and</u> outcome with a logical plan to sequentially interrupt each part of the process.

Rather than solving fundamental problems that would lead to solutions, a hyper-expensive *cycle of maintenance* has evolved using a stove-pipe or silo approach. This is when each *outcome* is separated and targeted by *specialists* with little regard to out-of-specialty influences or manifestations. It is not geared to solution as the practitioner employs a silo analysis and solution approach. Thus the multi-millions going to the latest so-called "best practices" are not effective as they structurally fail to take into account the humane need for a systemic, comprehensive and multi-targeted process that would in fact end childhood bloodshed. This may be because the "best practices" come from the society that brought you gangs in the first place. It is in no way holistic or in any way effective treatment of a widespread malady. It is self-serving at best for career and self-aggrandizement. An honest approach would incorporate the science of logical analysis (analytics) and work toward integration of research and subsequent strategies with complete and total *solution* as the only desired outcome.

In the classic **cycle of maintenance**, police, jails, prisons, injunctions, welfare, probation and unemployment centers become locked in place around now formally targeted communities. The criminal justice system grows tentacles around the community, their readily identifiable 'wayward' youth and their families. Management is now as complete as is possible in a free society. There is no thoughtful analysis applied in this paradigm as it is reactive. In the absence of a logical and scientific protocol, programs that "shoot from the hip" often suffice as "preventative". And sometimes the efforts to save young people do more harm than good.

In L.A. County, a Probation Department "prevention program" targeted youth from gang areas, never convicted of a crime but were "acting out" in class. They were placed on Probation caseloads as a preventative measure. Their families were *contractually obligated* to go to the Probation Department for counseling where they and a parent sat in the same waiting room as hard-core felons. To complete their negative conditioning and reinforcement and preparation for their perceived future, these impressionable youngsters would go on field trips in grey county jail buses sitting on seats where blood, urine and feces may have been earlier in the day and peered out of wired and barred windows.

The plan was to "save" a few of what was assumed to otherwise become violent "hard-core" killers using such counseling and field trips but seemed more like a sick pre-adolescent version of "scared straight".

In "reservation communities" an army of paid professionals engage in profiling, indexing of a community's youth, limiting freedom of movement and association, disallowing symbols used (including religious), specialized policing, gang-sweeps based on appearance and location, developing rating systems and biological measures for violence potential, penalty enhancements requiring expanding jails and prisons and Internet monitoring and prosecution, ad infinitum. And these are all aimed at a people's youth.

Gang and violence cycles are reinforced by default

Outcomes are targeted while *origin* and *evolution* are not considered relevant. Prisons and jails are violence and crime learning centers. Other targeting actions reinforce the underlying belief that the violent behaviors are innate and permanent and children of color and culture are to blame for all of it.

These methods and supportive "research" have evolved an industry dedicated to what has become a symbiotic maintenance program whose existence relies on sustaining a **Self-reinforcing Feedback Loop**. *This maintenance of effort does not go to the source or evolution of community violence.*

When such "war" efforts inevitably fail, in city after city, more of the same is added. Or we hear the hopeless refrain to "give up on this generation and concentrate on the next". The classic and revealing call that exposes the actual process involved - *a process that effectively condemns each new group of young people to traditional patterns that generate intolerable amounts of rage that leads to **their** destruction, containment and removal in turn as the community continues to be targeted with high-cost and ultimately ineffective occupation, enforcement and concentrated suppression tactics.*

Targeted communities fall victim to local, rage-generated violence and efforts to suppress the violence in a true **Societal Cycle of Violence** that guarantees structural adversity to overcome and many forms of violence for "reservation community" residents and especially children, to fall victim to.

There is a dramatic difference in how "reservation communities" are treated vs. European gang youth, i.e., White Supremacists Nazis, KKK, Skinheads and other ersatz hate-groups. As example, a strict, Zero Tolerance policy has been adopted by the FBI and local law enforcement to catch, prosecute and lock-up youthful minority "criminals-to-be" when "caught" making a gang hand-sign or wearing a cap or color of clothing (including on the Internet). Meanwhile, the Nazis and KKK groups have uniforms, a well- advertised hate and elimination policy toward identified groups of color and culture, hand and arm signals and a proven record of murder and mayhem yet *are not targeted in any form of Zero Tolerance or other such punitive policy.* The authoritative agency that monitors these groups is the Southern Poverty Law Center, Intelligence Project which can only monitor their activity but has no enforcement authority or linkages to law enforcement.

All youth violence demands action. If taken to logical ends, current policies combined with ongoing patterns of street violence would eventually result in all youth in a "reservation community" eventually being eliminated by premature death, long-term incarceration, injury and/or related illnesses. Sadly, this appears to already be the case in many places.

Research tells us that morbidity and mortality rates are already consistently higher in "reservation communities". However, that is where research stops. Some of this sad outcome is certainly due to negative social modifications that have become usual. To the extent that we have created conditions that induce violence and early death and the manner we have prosecuted this "war" we have to honestly ask, **"what is it that we truly desire as the end-game?"**

In order for such an appalling process to remain in place there must be significant benefit to someone or it would not exist. Since it is so atrocious a process, it must remain mysterious or be disguised in order to remain acceptable at all. The people destroyed by it must be made to believe that all of it is their own doing. And those who benefit would also need to believe the same in order to remain distanced and blameless from the process. It appears we are on track with all of these.

These objectives are seeded in the ***Social Conditioning*** and the ***Adaptation*** phases where beliefs are the underlying force; where negative acts and propaganda reinforce multi-generational bias and hatred of others *and of self.* Belief is a source of action. Some beliefs promote positive

124

action and others negative. Children learn and form beliefs about themselves and others based on what they see, hear and experience.

Negative beliefs about "reservation communities" have been created and passed along as folklore and tradition requiring no validation or confirmation. Some come to believe that a group's negative outcomes are a function of a people's existence and is as permanent as their existence. This includes gang folklore: the "once upon a time" stories whereby certain persons started this gang or that.

Such a belief system is a form of violence. Children are *positively* guided about the majority group and *negatively* guided about minority groups, helping assure continuity of positive and negative outcomes *according to group.* As belief become action, tradition and then history, groups act from a subconscious and constantly reinforced belief indoctrination, until and unless such indoctrination is changed.

15

Civil Unrest and Civil Upheaval
Gangs to Riots

Sometimes the process spins out of control. The lid comes off in a thousand fragments and everyone pays attention. Police say the gangs did it. Civic leaders downplay it. Talking heads are everywhere and analyses flow like a stock market ticker and media has a field day. But for years there were signs and signals. For years the "rioting" was waged at a lower ebb. And it still goes on all around you and me. We just don't realize the true nature of unrest and upheaval. For the dynamics are the same save for degree.

...all community violence is "rioting" - the type, level and duration are a matter of degree, dictated by particular circumstances...

<u>Civil Unrest</u> and <u>Civil Upheaval</u>

➢ *Civil Unrest* and *Civil Upheaval* are only separated by level and degree but connected as a reactionary process to externally initiated antagonisms.

A state of ***unrest*** is the accepted "natural" state for a "reservation community". ***Upheaval*** is the occasional riot and is always noticeable outside the community so must be explained.

➢ Traditionally, *unrest and upheaval* have been presented as gang initiated and peculiar to a group and community.

Riots are a community's ultimate expression of widespread anger and rage and overwhelming dissatisfaction with the status quo. And all efforts at keeping the two worlds hermetically separated have failed. Containment and control are no longer possible and the lid has been blown off. Rioting, like gangs, is a misunderstood aspect of community violence.

Gangs are most often blamed for riots even though post-riot investigative commissions conclude that social, economic and political issues are consistently the *underlying causes* of such uprisings. *The same is true of gangs.* Riots and gangs **are** connected... *but as effects not as causes.*

The so-called "Rodney King Riots" seemed to be out of context with modern-day America. The size and scope of the latest riots brought home the realization that America continues to be out of touch with its minority communities. The average American seemed surprised that in this day and age such a conflagration was even possible.

However, it became dreadfully apparent that some communities were powder kegs, ready to explode with simmering rage as palpable as ever.

A Black Epiphany

"...but you can't fool all of the people all of the time".

Abraham Lincoln

It is all **unrest** and **upheaval.** Gang activity is rioting but at a lower level. Generally speaking, violence in "reservation communities" usually remains at moderate levels. Triggers are everywhere and implosions are redundant.

However, on occasion, groups have reached the highest level on the Peace and Violence Continuum as during the 1960's and again in 1992 when rioting occurred in Los Angeles and other parts of the nation. Community violence is given major attention when communities move beyond *implosion* to *explosion.* At the riot level, community violence touches everyone in one way or another. Barring such explosion however, gangs are left to "riot" amongst themselves.

Case in Point: The Riots Last Time...

The April, 1992 upheaval in Los Angeles and other cities provides examples of several related dynamics in motion and coming to a head. Some occurred over time and others simultaneously. The riots shouldn't have surprised anyone. Gasoline was on the streets of Los Angeles and places like it. Rodney King was merely the lighted match that triggered *this* explosion.

The rise of anger and rage among a group relies on a constant feed of real and perceived *unjustified* violent acts being perpetrated *against them as a group* that, like gangs and other extraordinary reacting, only a society has the capability to perpetrate and allow. The build-up to the Rodney King verdict was given explosive dressing by separate but related factors and unless one looks closely, the obvious is missed.

The incidents leading up to the rioting are fundamentally no different than what occurs in slow and excruciating ways on a daily basis in "reservation communities" across America. However, incidents are usually spread over time and various locations so go largely uncounted as potentially leading to riotous upheaval. An explosion with the magnitude of a riot serves to overshadow the pertinent incidents that lead up to them. Such incidents have a cumulative impact on a people and result in various types of lower level unrest (implosions).

However, eventually critical mass is reached and tipping points are breached resulting in self-destructive modes (imploding), then peer annihilation (imploding) and ultimately all-out conflagration (exploding).

During a riot, regardless of the group involved, the action-reaction chain of events is instantaneous in comparison to the decades of slow, painful movement preceding it.

Leading up to 1992 (as was also the case in the 1960's and earlier riots), the steady economic, social and political violence and social exclusion aimed at "reservation communities" were constant. Efforts to gain power and redress were violently put down and leaders dealt with as criminals and anarchists. As some parts of society bragged, "he with the most toys wins", in "reservation communities" basic needs were harder to come by. Frustration, anger and rage were palpable. Society ignored the steady up-tick of inward directed anger that was most severe in black "reservations".

The upward spiraling black-on-black violence was the most significant clue that an outward explosion of some magnitude was on the horizon as the decade of the 80's had been the deadliest to date. Family abuse, drug use, murder and welfare rates climbed as did unemployment and drop-out rates. In addition to self-destructive behaviors were violent deaths of African-Americans at the hands of non-African-Americans. The shooters were exonerated in courts of white law *but not in the court of black social history.* These pieces of the pattern all pointed to the upward limits of toleration having been reached in black "reservations" across America.

At about the same time, there began a perceived take-over of black communities by non-black families and businesses. Media was unrelenting in its depiction of blacks as society's major predators and losers responsible for gangs, crime, welfare and drug proliferation, and typical of the day, no one officially gave a damn. And with each upward tick, more young lives were tossed onto the pyre. This all occurred leading up to April, 1992.

Lifetimes of rage were ready to be unleashed at the next insult. When the Rodney King incident occurred, fuses that were scattered thick were again lit. When the verdict came, all hell broke loose. The crack of the camel's back could be heard around the world and the white-hot inferno was on.

As the trial verdict began to seal our fate, the Black response was immediate. The dam had burst and out poured the same water-torture droplets but now blasting forth as avenging torrents of violent rage. The flow was caustic as were the containers holding it. Businesses were burning and looting had begun. Civil upheaval was on and for real, straight from the bowels of urban grief now turned to blinding vengeance.

During the massive release of the riot, some fundamental group dynamics changed. Unless fully processed and understood, the violence appears as nothing more than flames of rage for a verdict gone wrong.

The Epiphany

For many Crip and Blood enemy soldiers, their self-hate warfare was transformed in an instant. Angry youth were forced to process their emotions and anger as once avowed adversaries stood side-by-side venting their common wrath. They experienced as an epiphany the realization that their rage was not blue rage or red, not Crip rage or Blood, not Eastside or Westside. There were too many players from both sides and all sides letting loose generations of rage. A new truth was illuminated by these flames of anger. They realized in an instant that they were all victims of a far greater adversary than gang turf or colors or gang war this or that. The lie was exposed – and it also was thrown down on the burning pyre of rage, fed by the same fuel that up to the day before had sealed many a brother's end. Their violent responses were no longer aimed at each other. It now became directed outward and away. However, the sources of rage were still pounding away, harder than ever and the anger would continue to be released until those levels receded to a safer point - until next time.

As the flames grew so did the violence. People were pulled from cars and trucks with the same murderous hatred previously saved for brothers. The rage was electric, blinding all sense of humanitarian judgment. Racial epithets spewed everywhere and on everyone. A white truck driver was beaten senseless; a Latin man was doused with lighter fluid and about to be set on fire but the lighter failed and out of nowhere came an African-American man of God who jumped in the breach saving the Latino's life.

African-Americans, Latino, Anglo and Asian brothers and sisters attacked and counter-attacked. All lost loved ones and livelihoods. Every group seemed to be at war with every other group. Victims were everywhere. Many were killed and injured, nameless to the avenger. Everyone was a potential gang member and victim.

As non-response became law, individuals of different races joined in the looting, violence and mayhem. Chaos and need drove the day. Christmas had come early; enforcement too late. Even white youth made hay, burning LAPD in effigy and some buildings on the grounds of LAPD headquarters. Yet they remained strangely safe from police vengeance. As the rioting progressed, Rodney King was the last person on people's minds. His plea for everyone to please get along fell on deaf ears. His role had ended.

This is a recent example of a community reaching maximum Level V, <u>Civil Upheaval</u> on the Peace and Violence Continuum. The primary affected group this time was African-American, which triggered other groups already at various stages of *unrest* verging on *upheaval*. And once again, there were tremendous losses to the community, the region and the nation in lives, resources and pride. Such are the heavy costs of our social order.

Rage can only build so much before it overflows beyond established containers. We should not be surprised when it blows up in our faces as happens in a full-blown conflagration. In the past, the Irish, Jews and Italians raged out of control. This time it was once again African-Americans that were pushed to explosive levels. They had long ago passed beginning stages and hovered at moderate levels for two decades until pieces again fell into place by continuing to fall apart.

Riots are cyclical – and as permanent as gangs.

There is *always* a "riot" going on – in the homes on the streets and in the schools in "reservation communities". Some groups are at the build-up stage, some at moderate levels and some ready to ignite. The type, method and magnitude are no different from place to place and group to group, whether Latino, Native American, Filipino, Samoan, Vietnamese, Russian, Armenian, or African-American, or Salvadoran, Nicaraguan, Puerto Rican, Cuban or Mexican, or...

132

To date, we have opted not to delve too deeply into aspects behind such events as long as the "rioting" remains in "reservation communities". However, it is only a matter of time and circumstance that any group reaches critical mass that ends at explosive aggression, be it an actual riot, a gang drive-by or shooting up a school. *These manifestations are as permanent as the conditions that spawn them and will recur as long as conditions remain that induce such outcomes.*

Just as the build-up of gangs is directly related to negative societal conditions during their social history, so are riots. *If conditions are such that a gang(s) forms and ignites into warfare, "rioting" is begun. Societal conditions will determine the size, type and duration of their presence and activity. The same is true of explosive conflagrations (riots). If conditions do not improve, once a riot has been quelled, the build-up to the next one begins.* This is the overarching <u>*cycle of social violence.*</u>

The critical mass build-up to a riot is the same as the critical mass build-up to gang and other community violence. It is all a matter of degree. **A full-blown conflagration (riot) is triggered somewhere beyond gang violence.** Riots also have their tipping points that have everything to do with societal elements and relationships between society and a group, and, contrary to popular belief, *have nothing to do with gangs.* Both are outcomes of a similar process. And just as *gangs do not cause more gangs, riots do not cause more riots.* Neither are riots intrinsically *multigenerational* nor *part of a people's culture* or *in their genes.* Neither are they caused by *colors* or *turf* or *status* or *respect* or *revenge* or *graffiti.* And they will not end if we *give up on this generation and concentrate on the next.* Not even if a roomful of scientists continue to follow the eugenics path and somehow "prove" that ethnic youth are genetically "hardwired" for violence. This myopic viewpoint can only lead to medicating and/or locking-up every "reservation community" child who acts out but will not prevent the riot next time. We have to start from scratch and do it all the right way *for a change.* **The same issues that create riots create gangs and other violence sub-cycles**. Violence critical mass including gang activity manifests with types and levels of **societal** unrest and upheaval.

As successful equality and integration occur, community violence at all levels dissipates.

A *"cycle of riots"*

Except for the so-called Rodney King riots, rioting in the past had done little to effect change. The lack of positive movement brought more frustration and the gap between Black and White widened.

Since the Watts Riot in 1965, a *riot cycle* began anew for the African-American. Nothing changed to prevent future rage build-up from starting all over again – and to a future explosion. Later in that same decade, Latinos and Native Americans marched and demonstrated against racism and inequality, and were routed by authorities as peaceful demonstrations were violently put down. Their level of internalized unrest (gangs) then took a jump and remains as violent forms of *imploding*. They have not reached critical mass necessary for *explosion* (riot) and so are left to implode "quietly". The violence here lingers at moderate levels but they are "rioting" nonetheless.

The 1980's were extraordinarily tumultuous and in 1992, the build-up again reached a zenith and spilled over to a massive explosion level. This time it left a trail that some learned from, thank God. This time, some basic changes occurred which should delay or even prevent the next conflagration at least in African-American communities. Still, not enough has changed to end lower level "rioting" there or in the many other "reservation communities". And children killing children remains an American horror story.

White Youth Rioting?

The feeling of social, political and economic uneasiness is a relatively new experience for growing numbers of the white population. More children than ever are out in that same heartless cold, and in single parent homes and as latchkey children. They feel the effects of an unfriendly economy and other seemingly *unjustified* external pressures on their families, albeit not over decades and generations. Children don't understand their new reality. They are beginning to feel powerless, alienated, uncared for, excluded and resentful - *the first stages of marginalization.*

Desperation, paranoia and depression add pressure to the mix. As white youth try to insulate themselves, the same social toxins as have affected "reservation communities" over generations take their toll. Some abuse substances and join with small bands of reactive groups and/or form new ones. This is the **Hybrid Gang** that has joined and in some cases replaced, the **Traditional Gang,** if you will, as host and crucible for this new youth evolution and potential revolution. Social modifications and compensation methods will evolve; susceptibility to relatively minor acts and insults increase; sub-economies form. There will then be those 'black sheep' at the margins as in "reservation communities" who are not necessarily going through a "phase of growing up" as the National Gang Center (NGC) wants us to believe to dismiss their drug involvement, group violence and property destruction. If they feel under attack (and it need only be a feeling), they will locate a suitable blame-target for reprisal and release.

Youth that are already or believe they are about to become disenfranchised may react with anger and resentment. Anger covers a pained existence that eventually becomes unbearable. At a point a release mechanism comes into play. Thus, involvement of youth not traditionally related to violence or gangs increases. This completion aspect of the overarching **_cycle of social violence_** has the society feeling the effects of youth violence *within the majority population group, directly and painfully* – and they unwittingly join an end-game not meant for them. Thus the **cycle of violence** becomes a **_circle_ _of violence_**, beginning and ending at everyone's door.

The outburst against multiple targets as happened in Columbine, Colorado, was carried out by white youth against a primarily white youth population. In this case they made their own makeshift blame-targeting rules. However, the killers fit the gang prerequisite of first believing and accepting that they were themselves outcasts and marginalized. The need for rage-release produced the same violent result and expressed itself as self-hate turned outward as hate. They adopted a gang model as they separated from society. They even had their own "colors": black. They then manufactured an enemy from within their midst and bang, bang, you're dead.

Some youth will join traditional gang movements such as the **Predator Gangs**; others form new groupings with other groups (**Hybrid Gangs**). Still others form their own ersatz version to fill an immediate perceived void (e.g. Columbine incident). The **Hate Gang** also sees a marked increase as some youth perceive a need to be *race-protective*. These as well as **Same-Group** gangs are discussed in-depth in Volume 2.

Non-ethnic white youth may become violent as a power move - a reaction to a real or perceived threat to the power and standing of their group. They may act as a gang motivated partly by anger but also to control and contain other group(s) by acts designed to bring generalized terror to the offending population(s) – to teach them a lesson. When a white group feels the threat of a minority, a representative set may act as the agent (gang) of the whole. They believe their act represents popularly held beliefs of their community.

Included in this group is the *ad-hoc* **Hate Gang** that does violence as a group in spur of the moment acts against a minority person. In this example, *race-protective* groupings believe their larger group is harmed by the expanding promise of freedom and opportunity. They may become resentful to the point of race targeting. The victim(s) picked for rage-release will be already tagged as social outcast, e.g., a contemporary minority. In these situations the stage is set by society's active negative beliefs and biases. Thus, this ad-hoc gang has "social support" lent by politicians, media and contemporary "leaders" sufficient to use blame-targeting to justify an act(s) of violence. The assumption is the punishment will not be too great.

Minorities of all types have borne the brunt of such rage-release events. Historically, acts have included lynching, spur of the moment deadly beatings, gang rapes, dragging to death behind a vehicle, etc. *Ad-hoc* **Hate Gangs** act based on what they believe are their larger group's beliefs.

Another example occurred in Chicago, 1919. From the Chicago Public Library, *"On the afternoon of July 27, 1919, Eugene Williams, a black youth, drowned off the 29th Street beach. A stone throwing melee between blacks and whites on the beach prevented the boy from coming ashore safely. After clinging to a railroad tie for a lengthy period, he drowned when he no longer had the strength to hold on"*. This was the finding of the Cook County Coroner's Office after an inquest was held into the cause of death.

William Tuttle, Jr.'s book, *Race Riot: Chicago in the Red Summer of 1919*, includes a 1969 interview with an eyewitness. The witness was one of the boys swimming and playing with Eugene Williams in Lake Michigan between 26th Street and the 29th Street Beach who recalled having rocks thrown at them by a single White male standing on a breakwater 75 feet from their raft. Eugene was struck in the forehead and as his friend attempted to aid him, Eugene panicked and drowned. The man on the breakwater left, running toward the 29th Street Beach. By this time rioting had already erupted there precipitated by vocal and physical demonstrations against a group of blacks who wanted to use the beach in defiance of its tacit designation as a "white" beach. The rioting escalated when a white police officer refused to arrest the white man, by now identified as the perpetrator of the separate incident near 26th Street. Instead he arrested a black individual. Anger over this, coupled with rumors and innuendos that spread in both camps regarding Eugene Williams's death led to 5 days of rioting in Chicago that ultimately claimed the lives of 23 blacks and 15 whites, with 291 wounded and maimed. There are similar examples in our history as we know too well.

Our history has included white supremacist gang activity and rioting of every kind and degree. Whether white youth get liquored up enough to seek out a person of color, mimic the more traditional gangster mode or retreat under white bed sheets, their trip can turn deadly.

In addition to racial motivations, the "threat" pressure may be general such as when affirmative action, equal housing and employment are advanced. Violence up to and including rioting to control non-white groups may arise as they seek to "put them back in their place" and out of societal competition. This may occur when control mechanisms are suddenly reversed such as court ordered publically funded school attendance; reversals of discriminatory hiring and promotion practices; forced equalized housing and lending practices; forced equalized education such as funding books, computers and educators in minority schools.

In any case, under some circumstances, non-ethnic whites will have fringe or extremist elements of their group (gangs) acting "on behalf" of the group just as the minority gang "black sheep" does within their group. These are wars at the societal level and battles are ongoing in politics and courtrooms. The outcomes can be the beginning to community peace or a portent to future violence.

Gangs (and riots) can result from real and perceived inequities among peoples. They act inversely to unresolved social conflict among and between groups. They act in place of their larger group population. Each "army" is reacting to social forces already in play and that are much larger than the individual and their violent group – they are merely reactive vessels.

The shock of a riot event invites all manner of reasoning, speculation and justification that, like gangs, runs the gamut. Biases become blatantly interspersed with social realities. As is the case with gangs and other violent sub-cycles, those in power tend to look at the *event* and not the *context* of the event. Disagreement, misunderstanding and confusion hamper solutions that **could mitigate gangs and riots**, especially since they occur in the same communities. In order to begin to better understand the sequential dynamics and to separate *origin* from *evolution* and *outcome*, a new look at terminology and meaning is proposed:

Unrest, Upheaval and Rioting…

A ***Riot*** is described as a unique event whereby community members are moved to set fires, vandalize and loot property and businesses, assault and murder persons. ***Civil unrest*** and ***civil upheaval*** are both used to describe such "rioting". A ***cycle of violence*** is described as a unique community condition whereby youth kill other youth without end or justification.

There exists a perceived distinction between local *cycles of violence*, e.g. *gangs*, and widespread community uprisings, e.g. *riots, unrest and upheaval when in fact there is no such distinction. It is all a matter of sequence and degree.*

Nor is there an separation with other forms of elevated community violence, e.g. elevated levels of family abuse, substance abuse, suicides, bullying, etc. Community-wide uprisings (riots, revolts, insurrections, rebellions) share the same dynamics as other kinds of community violence that ranges from elevated levels of various abuses to gang violence. ***All are relative states of community unease, agitation, turmoil and disorder.***

The terms, *unrest* and *upheaval* invoke similar responses leading to the same closed-end conclusions…just as does "gang cycle of violence". They all are used to describe a terminal condition reached *within* a "reservation community".

It is suggested the same terms be applied in describing the *external sources* of the internalized volatile condition, i.e., the *external to internal (violence) dynamic* that leads to the *internal to external (violence) response*.

The differences and variances are a matter of degree existing on the same plane and on the same *societal continuum*. Each must be better delineated for context and relationship in a volatile environment in order that the entire dynamic may be better understood and then appropriately analyzed and treated. The point can be made to contextualize terms for use on a historical *peace and violence continuum*.

In regards to the gangs and community violence dynamic, a more definitive categorization is proposed…one that is integrated and helps define relationship and magnitude of *origin, evolution* and *outcome*.

Civil Unrest and *Civil Upheaval*

Civil Unrest: The chronic state of disturbance and unease that exists between a society and certain homogeneous groups *and* among and between groups. The sources and supports may be both *external* and *internal* to community but manifests as *relatively lower levels of violence*.

Two forms of *Civil Unrest*:

1. ***Societal Violence***

2. ***Community Violence***

Societal Violence:

That overt and covert violence that emanates from societal beliefs, traditions, self-interests and practices detrimental to a group(s). *Societal Violence* includes marginalization, exploitation, dehumanization that includes resource deficiencies in fundamental areas necessary to secure basic needs and to advance *within* a society. It also includes certain physical violence emanating as a consequence of those same societal beliefs, self-interests, traditions and practices.

Societal Violence includes social, economic, environmental and political acts, laws and policies that have negative impacts on certain homogeneous communities, from redlining to racially motivated beatings by ad hoc gangs, and certain acts that may be interpreted as bias related by authority.

These elements of externally generated *civil unrest* initiate and reinforce multigenerational resentment, frustration, anger and eventual potential to violence and help underpin "reservation community" creation and evolution.

Community Violence:

The corresponding, elevated and repeated violent *reaction(s)* and *response(s)* emanating from within and usual to a homogenous community *as a result of* directed **Societal Violence.**

Community Violence results from shared negative experiences to the extent that corresponding release and reactive mechanisms become usual. This violence consists of localized destruction done to self, within families, among peers and to local community. Activities include bullying, fistfights, gang formation and attendant illegal activity and vandalism. Negative social and economic factors may result in *social modifications* that include illegal sub-economic ventures. Patterns and cycles of substance abuse form and the community experiences chronically elevated unemployment, family violence, school drop-out and welfare rates.

This phase of **civil unrest** is a community *imploding* from elements of **societal violence**. The process emanates from *outside* a community with effects manifesting *inside* the community. External *and* internal violence processes support negative patterns and cycles. This is the "reservation community" imploding. Both processes eventually become institutionalized (cyclic) and feed inter-community violence. They are cumulative, progressive and destructive to community and ultimately the society. Patterns of **Community Violence** do not end until **Societal Violence** is ended.

Over time, community *unrest* eventuates to a permanent ebb and flow dynamic *(cycles of violence)* bounding dangerously close to explosion. This origin and evolutionary process becomes evident on a Peace and Violence Continuum. Points on the chart illustrate how a community trends to Peace or Violence...*and occasional explosion.*

Civil Upheaval:

Civil Upheaval is that explosion...the advanced or cataclysmic violence affecting what will become or has evolved to a "reservation community". These also include external and internal processes. However, **civil**

upheaval also describes the violent introduction, clashing of cultures and conquering process.

Two phases of <u>Civil Upheaval</u>:

1.   *Societal Calamity*

2.   *Community Upheaval*

Societal Calamity:

The calamitous, devastatingly violent attack(s) directed against a group, community or person(s) representing a group. *Societal Calamity* includes lynching and massacres, violent attacks and raids that involve burning, beating, rape and murder. *Societal Calamity* includes mass relocation/deportation and extraordinary and selective abuse by authorities.

These are blatant, violent surges of destruction affecting the core of a community that are socially and/or government led, driven, sanctioned and/or allowed, overtly and covertly. Sources are *external* to community but under certain related circumstances *can combine* with escalating *internal* processes to produce riotous conflagration and explosion.

Actions and events on both sides inflict fear and terror in individuals, groups and communities as some are indeed acts of terrorism. Socially driven calamitous acts sear the souls of a people and become a part of their unwritten social history. Over time, these also invite formation of reactive practices and then *cycles of violence* first directed inward at lower levels as *community violence* against peers, family and community. However, the degree of damage done at this stage can produce all levels of unrest and upheaval, including **riots**.

The forceful government response is demanded. However, in and of itself a continuous paramilitary response can become a form of perpetual community maintenance and control. Structural solutions become secondary by virtue of military expenditures. This process is then repetitive (cyclic) as long as source and evolutionary formats remain in place.

> ➤ *Societal Calamity* generates *massive* internal community anger, frustration, rage and *unrest* (gangs, etc.) and occasional *community upheaval* (riots).

Community Upheaval:

The riotous, uncontrolled conflagration that occurs within a homogeneous community profoundly affected by **Societal Violence** and **Societal Calamity.**

Community Upheaval can occur when a "reservation community" experiences elevated and prolonged negative treatment and finally explodes. A level of tolerance has been breached and the community can become engulfed in fires, destruction of property, gunfire and looting from within. This is a massive release of pent- up rage, usually triggered by an event at the *calamity* stage (beating, shooting, tragic arrest) seen as unjust and *unjustified* that occurs at the apex of tolerance…the last straw.

The Rodney King beating is freshest in memory. But there are literally thousands more.

Two classic incidents representative of **Societal Upheaval** occurred recently in Texas. One to an African-American man and then a few years later to a Latino youth who was attacked by white supremacists. *"…they beat the student, shoved a piece of PVC pipe into the young man's rectum, and then plowed it deep into his organs by kicking it. One attacker wore a steel-toed boot. They also tried to carve on his chest, stomped on his head and poured bleach over him, yelling Hispanic slurs throughout the attack. He lay in the yard for 10 hours."* (Kansas City Star; May 09, 2006).

This occurred a few years after an African-American man was tied behind a pick-up truck and dragged to death, also by a gang of white youths in Texas. The Latino youth later committed suicide. These were done by civilians and in the case of the Latino male, the attackers were teenagers. These kinds of incidents still occur and are universally minimized by prosecutors, juries and by local media.

Another classic form of **societal upheaval** occurred to a 91 year old grandmother, her family and thus her "reservation community":

ABBEVILLE, Alabama — The mayor of a southeast Alabama town and a state legislator are apologizing to relatives of a black woman raped in 1944 by a gang of white men: "Abbeville Mayor Ryan Blalock expressed his sorrow to relatives of Recy Taylor during a news conference today. The woman's brother and several other relatives attended.

Now ninety-one years old, Taylor was 24 and living in her native Henry County when she was gang-raped in Abbeville in 1944. The married woman was walking home from church when she was abducted, assaulted and left on the side of the road in an isolated area.

Two all-white, all-male grand juries declined to bring charges. State Rep. Dexter Grimsley of Newville says police bungled the investigation and harassed Taylor. Police tried to blame her family who were threatened and their home firebombed.

Today, this incident may well trigger *community upheaval* as did the Rodney King beating.

Although a decades-later apology is sad compensation for the trauma and ruination of a young woman and her family, this and similar incidents were brought to light by proper research, thus discovery that then resulted in a book (*At The Dark End of The Street*; *Danielle McGuire*) which then became actionable.

We readily accept that gang violence and rioting are levels of **unrest** and **upheaval**. But so are the massacres, lynch mobs, raids, gang rapes, brutal beatings, forced removal and sanctioned and excused murder. All are contained within a larger social process and contained in every affected group's social history. **Unrest** and **upheaval** are levels of violence on a continuum and connected to the group "body" as by an umbilical cord.

➢ **On a <u>Peace and Violence Continuum,</u> *<u>Civil Unrest</u>* and *<u>Civil Upheaval</u>* are interrelated social phenomenon.**

➢ **Research does not examine evidence for a possible connection in these areas.**

Following ***Community Upheaval*** (riot), community unease will retreat to previous levels of ***unrest***, albeit still relatively elevated. In absence of societal modifications to improve underlying conditions, localized violent activity resumes as before. The entire community violence dynamic is reported as emanating from a few bad actors responsible for the gangs *and* the riots. And they only occur in the "reservation community". The society ceases its concern thus guaranteeing the volatile process *will again* become re-energized and move slowly and inexorably to ***upheaval*** (riot) level.

"Reservation communities" are in a perpetual state of *unrest* with occasional periods of *upheaval* – both from without and within. However, we must include the forms of violence emanating from the society. Therefore, when a city council, school board, county board, state body or even a Supreme Court approves and/or upholds racial segregation, unequal education, selectively applied voter rules, relegated community amenities (schools, parks, libraries, open space), they are engaging in *unrest;* When members of minorities are illegitimately denied home loans or employment, the agent, the lending institution and the employer are engaging in *unrest;* when a group of minority children are profiled as gang members due to skin color and where they live, the law is engaging in *unrest;* when a vigilante group of citizens intimidates to prevent a minority adult from registering to vote or voting, or a child from attending a school they are engaging in *unrest;* and when young people from these communities then begin to act out community anger and frustration, they are engaging in *unrest.* One can go down a history of laws, policies, acts and behaviors where citizens, institutions and representatives of institutions engage in *societal unrest* – a process that leads to *community unrest* and eventual *upheaval.*

A much dismissed facet is again, white youth gang violence. This is the racist skinhead and KKK member who attacks non-white persons. They are considered a political group and social movement and not classified as a violent gang, nor are their gang actions classified as gang activity. Or their behaviors are considered "transitory" and not formal "gang" actions. Regardless of dress, behavior or actions they are not subjected to active profiling and other "reservation community" monitoring, enforcement or prosecutorial enhancements or tactics. Their protected existence may be due to ignorance but also tacit approval. They act on behalf of what they believe the larger population believes and desires. If the record of easy justice and lax punishments is a guide, they may have a point.

A need to continue to remake and *improve* America

There may no longer be massacres like a Wounded Knee, the East St. Louis, Ill. Massacre (July 2, 1917), a Circleville Massacre (July, 1866) or the many similar events. But many incidents of overt violent acts of terrorism have been directed at targeted communities in many places but not paid attention to outside those communities. Persons living there know that this kind of extreme violence is directed at their population. While these incidents are now occasional, they are still overt **source** forms of violence that account for a perpetual state of simmering anger that illicit local **unrest** and **upheaval** in the forms of gangs and riots.

Part 3

The Crimson Flow...

...blood, guts and war trauma

16

The Crimson Flow

Violence on a people whether by gun, economic, social or political racism is still violence regardless of weapons used. All violence is potentially traumatic and has consequences not adequately taken into account as origins of community violence. These foundational elements may not be seen as such but their consequences are deeply felt. The primary response is internal, affecting esteem and outlook on life. Violence also affects the health of the individual. Once subjected to a negative event or series of events, an individual, family, community and a people can experience an alteration in their psyches and well-being. Such trauma can manifest in many ways. Being aware of this connection can help in understanding how a child can move away from being a loving human being. At some point a local cycle of violence kicks in with its own set of life altering events. The combination can be devastating.

At an elementary school in a Los Angeles suburb, I was observing our Star-Kids Program classroom discussion on the impact on family members when one belongs to a gang. While other children raised their hands and joined in the discussion one child kept looking out the window and down at his desk. I will call him William. During a break I eased over, sat on the floor and asked him how he was doing?

He did not reply but stared down or at the corner of his desk. After a minute he looked at me for a split second. With watery eyes he began to speak very softly of how much he missed his brother. He told of watching his brother die sitting a few feet from him during dinner. At times almost imperceptibly, he described how bullets burst through the kitchen wall and with his hand moving to his face, pointed to where a bullet entered his brother's mouth and how the whole back of his brother's head exploded and splattered the refrigerator. He said the house is always dark and that his mother cries all the time. He said he did not cry like his mother. I touched his shoulder but I don't think he felt it. He had said what was on his mind, what was troubling him. There was nothing that his teacher or I could do. It was early but William was done, and like many that I met in my work, his childhood was over.

Another day, I attended a graduation of our Star-Kids program at another elementary school in Los Angeles. This was to be a special event because one youngster, Rebecca, was returning to the school for the graduation and was to be honored by her classmates. She had been shot in the abdomen while walking to class and would wear a plastic bag on the side of her body for the rest of her shortened life. Although her mother had since moved the family to another area, she brought her to school to graduate the success oriented anti-gang program.

As her name and story were recounted, I noticed the tears in some of the student's eyes as well as the teachers. I also noticed hardness on some children's faces. As she received a standing ovation I felt a familiar sadness. Though Rebecca had triumphed, it was over an unrelenting violence that was and is central to the lives of many of America's youth. It was not a triumph understood or appreciated by the other America heretofore secure that their children would not experience such horror. But that was another time.

There are hundreds of thousands of Williams and Rebecca's in this great nation. Their stories reflect the life experience of many of our children who grow up in the war-torn parts of this nation. And warfare affects all directly or indirectly.

Children and war related trauma

Children do not learn well with bullets whizzing by, at least not the right lessons.

As violence shatters their emotional well being, desired channels of learning are blasted shut by the bloody explosions going off daily in their young faces. Eventually they close their eyes and cover their ears. These young people live different lives than youth in non-violent areas. While even one taste of brutality can mar a person for life, entire populations of young Americans are regularly exposed to mind-numbing violence. Many suffer a lifetime of crippling physical and psychological effects from encountering acts of extreme violence.

Young people raised in chronically high violence environments are subjected to several common negative experiences including sudden and violent deaths, physical and emotional injuries to family members and peers; self-destructive habits and behaviors; deaths due to suicide including 'accidental' suicides; and injury and deaths due to reckless behavior such as gun play. This is not a complete list. At a different level they experience emotionally jolting grief, guilt, anger, despair, fear and hopelessness. These young people are reacting to similar stimuli as children in war-torn third-world countries. Their young bodies live on but their souls are aged far beyond their years. They are at risk of deleterious side effects and may develop inferiority and other destructive complexes.

These children may report sleep disturbances, 'night sweats', insomnia, flashbacks to horrible events, thoughts of suicide and revenge. Some blame themselves for events. Some exhibit a lack of emotional responsiveness. Sometimes it comes across as inhibited learning ability. Stressful incidents and conditions do inhibit mental processes and intellectual development as well as contributing to serious health problems. They may likely and logically begin to believe they are different from everyone else and rather than blossom, begin to withdraw and shut down.

When violent experiences are combined with images of war and destruction too close to home, it becomes possible to imagine creating a monster, a perpetual victim, or both.

The children get the message that this is their lot. They receive a constant barrage of reinforcing negative propaganda declaring all of this is as it should be. A mutual estrangement is in place as the society and the child each adjust to this aspect of marginalization. But only the child of color becomes ill.

Violence causes stress. However, there are many forms of violence as pointed out. Racism is violence, and evidence is pointing to racism as causing stress and contributing to diseases, physical as well as psychological. Stress is a fight or flight response that sets chemical changes in motion. Stress alters healthy levels of triglycerides, adrenal hormones, blood pressure, cholesterol and other biological measures and has been linked to cardiovascular (heart) disease, diabetes, intestinal disorders, allergies, hives, insomnia, ulcers, skin disorders, sexual dysfunction and some cancers. People under constant stress may seek unhealthy ways to escape it and are thereby at risk of alcohol or drug abuse, overeating, smoking and other self-destructive behavior, including suicide. *("How Racism Hurts-Literally"; Madeline Drexler; Boston Globe; 7/15/07).*

During the late 1950's, Dr. Hans Selve, a pioneer in the study of stress stated, *"No organism can exist continuously in a state of alarm"*. The body is not designed to live in constant fear, danger and related stress. There may thus be a link between the higher than normal rates of heart, liver and other diseases among minority populations and stresses from *external* forces as well as inter-community forces.

Stress and aggression may be linked as well. According to the American Psychological Association (APA), stress and aggression reinforce each other at the biological level, creating a vicious cycle. (APAONLINE Oct. 10, 2004) Reporting on an article titled, *"Fast Positive Feedback Between the Adrenocortical Stress Response and a Brain Mechanism Involved in Aggressive*

Behavior" (Behavioral Neuroscience, Vol. 118, No. 5, Kruk, Meelis, Halasz, Haller, Oct. 2004), *"There appears to be a fast, mutual, positive feedback loop between stress hormones and a brain-based aggression-control center in rats, whose neurophysiology is similar to ours". "It may explain why, under stress, humans are so quick to lash out and find it hard to cool down".* The lead author states, *"It is well known that stress hormones, in part by mobilizing energy reserves, prepare the physiology of the body to fight or flee during stress. Now it appears the very same hormones 'talk back' to the brain in order to facilitate fighting".*

The article continued: *"in rapid order, stimulating the hypothalamic attack area led to higher stress hormones and higher stress hormones led to aggression, evidence of the feedback loop within a single conflict". "Such a mutual facilitation may contribute to the precipitation and escalation of violent behavior under stressful conditions".* They add that the resulting vicious cycle *"would explain why aggressive behavior escalates so easily and is difficult to stop once it has started, especially because corticosteroids rapidly pass through the brain barrier".*

The findings suggest that even when stress hormones spike for reasons not related to fighting, they may lower attack thresholds enough to precipitate violent behavior even for seemingly benign reasons. If this is found to be validated by additional research, it would help explain hyper-aggressive behavior in youth and others living in high-stress environments, even when in seemingly harmless settings.

Another study reported by the American Psychological Association, *(APAONLINE, August 2003),* reveals that a high number of American youth are exhibiting signs of Post Traumatic Stress Syndrome, (PTSD) and other stress related disorders. Reporting on an article titled, *"Violence and Risk of PTSD, Major Depression, Substance Abuse/ Dependence, and Comorbidity: Results From the National Survey of Adolescents,"* (Kilpatrick, Ruggiero, Acierno, Saunders, Resnick, Best in the Journal Of Consulting and Clinical Psychology, Vol. 71, No. 4.) *"The study, involving 4,023 youth (ages 12-17)... finds that roughly 16% of boys and 19% of girls met the criteria for at least one of the following diagnosis: PTSD, major depressive episode, and substance abuse/dependence". "Interpersonal violence (i.e., sexual and physical assault, witnessed violence) increased the risk of PTSD, major depressive episode, and substance abuse/dependence after controlling for demographic factors and family substance abuse problems, according to the study. This finding adds to the growing body of research establishing a link between interpersonal violence and mental health outcomes".*

Justifying an existence

To be sure, youth are severely harmed by the "reservation" experience and must be supported. Counseling and medication are being employed to treat symptoms but solutions lack a view to external causative elements of systemic community violence.

Some research links frustration to anger, aggression and to violence. One model posits that some individuals cannot or will not manage frustration, and at some cumulative point, frustration leads to feelings of anger, then aggression and a greater potential to violence. Another model links frustration to real or perceived underlying reasons for an adverse action. While these do not delve into the harsh "reservation community" environment, they are more on track with that reality.

In one model, aggression is variably related to *justified* and *unjustified* frustration (Berkowitz, Miller, Dollard, et al), i.e., if the *reason* for the frustration is seen by the individual as *justified,* aggressive behavior is reduced. If the reason is seen as *unjustified,* frustration and thus aggression is increased.

The theory's application appears limited to occurrences that have a direct cause and effect relationship, e.g., getting fired for constantly being late to work. In this case, one can (perhaps grudgingly) accept the logic of being fired as *justified* and thus frustration is reduced. However, if being fired is seen as *unjustified,* e.g., to replace him with a friend, this can lead to increased frustration, anger and greater likelihood of aggression and violence. But the research does not address the "reservation community" experience. This may be due to lack of research data as re: that experience. At any rate, finding *justification* for frustrations in "reservation communities" may be more difficult as a *logical* and/or *justifiable* basis for deleterious experiences is lacking.

Quality education that would lead to fulfilling employment and cultural and social resources may be lacking even in the same city without justification. Or the fact that it is more difficult to buy a home and obtain insurance at usual rates or at all. Why?

And much more serious and terrifying actions that defy logic and *justification* have occurred: family members and friends being hanged, dragged until dead, gang-raped, burned alive, shot, skinned alive, run out of town, burned out of their home, wrongly convicted of a crime, beaten up by mobs, etc. The victim group logically and rightly perceives these as *unjustified.* Unjustifiable social, economic, political and murderous violence is at the foundation of "reservation community" anger, rage and elevated potential to violence. The level of frustrations and anger are immeasurable by current standards. And the failure to reconcile the outcome with the cause has profound implications for healing. Youth are confused at best, and feel guilt, shame and responsibility for feelings they had no control over attaining. Nor can they logically explain or come to terms with them. But feel them, they do. *Unjustified* societal actions have been damaging to the point of being off the charts, and per Berkowitz' model, leads to higher levels of frustration, aggression and greater potential to violence.

A group's frustration – aggression level is more difficult to salve when actions are historically and incessantly unjustified as in a "reservation community". However, for accuracy in assessment and treatment a frustration/aggression/violence index should include this experience as elevated levels of frustration, anger and aggression should logically be present and be shown as difficult to manage. This might help explain bullying, the "chip on the shoulder" and other aggressive behaviors.

It would also seem to follow that to function within an illogical and unjustifiable environmental culture, social mores would modify to reflect the unjustified nature of that culture. Thus, gangs and other violent sub-cycles are "logical" outcomes of *unjustified* societal patterns and behaviors. They form *unjustifiable* rules and policies in response to *unjustifiable* conditions and realities.

A secondary consequence of continued *unjustified* social patterns and effects thereof is that over time, the negative response pattern becomes foundational to next generations.

Each new generation experiences elevated "baseline levels", if you will, of fear, frustration, anger, aggression, rage, etc., inherited from the cumulative past and by direct relationship with those earlier affected: role models who exhibit various methods of dealing with it all, good and bad. The shared everyday negative experiences become the usual and are accepted as part of an aberrant social existence. More simply, they go to sleep angry and wake up angry (and/or frustrated or other negative emotion), knowing by next day's end they will likely be insulted, disrespected, disfavored, shown disdain or even harmed physically by someone representing society *and/or* the local violent products of such societal machinations. Be it at school, work, while driving, boarding a plane, being in the "wrong" neighborhood, eating, applying for a job or a loan, renting an apartment, or watching a movie or TV show, their "baseline level" of fear, discomfort, frustration and anger is constantly being assaulted. Eventually internalized stress reaches harmful levels. The young person's mind, body and spirit have reached "overload" and left raw and threadbare. The violent response may be a self-preserving rejection of additional insult. The "short fuse" and "always angry and ready to fight" clichés may have relationship here as stressors exceed normal toleration levels.

At the same time in another part of town, youth are advancing, are learning more and accumulating more comforts, enjoying better lifestyles and succeeding in turn. And wondering what in the world is wrong with "those people"?

It might be enlightening to test how "reservation" residents respond to "normal" frustration as being *justified* or *unjustified*. The author suggests the "reservation" experience is unique in composition, severity and duration that traditional research does not adequately account for. E.g., the researcher describes events within a traditional, normative frustration

156

field; the "reservation" subject gives a response indicating how insignificant they perceive the frustrations presented (relative to their non-traditional and more intense experience) that places the "test" results at a relatively normal category. The researcher mistakenly concludes that "traditional" frustrations tested for are therefore within that class of individual's ability to handle and asks, 'so why are your people so angry and violent?' The test subject calmly explains to the well-meaning but uninformed researcher that he would happily live in this other world full of "traditional" frustrations…that in his world, frustrations are much more severe, beyond his control and *unjustified*. The researcher is at a loss to accept or explain such response as the area is not accounted for in experience, research or literature and is therefore, scientifically invalid. The fundamental disconnect is missed.

Research goes on without true understanding of the level and kinds of frustration or day to day realities experienced by the violence surrounded individual: violence from society *and* his own community. The two are related and hit like a one-two punch. Regardless, the reality is that the anger and violence are prevalent, longstanding and as permanent as that which causes it. Until then, we maintain a socially acceptable rationale that forces the reconciling of opposite realities…a rationale that dismisses societal violence as source, and places blame and responsibility on the group and their youth.

"Disorganized community" is the term used by the professional violence researcher, trainer and intervener to describe communities that experience youth violence as a norm, as well as high rates of poverty, crime, welfare, unemployment, school drop-outs, substance abuse, single parent households, unkempt neighborhoods, etc., ad nauseum. (www.sugeongeneral.gov/library/youthviolence/chapter4/sec3.html).
This term describes symptoms and outcomes and does nothing to enlighten as to how a community became "disorganized" or why it remains that way. It seems logical that a primary, formative relationship exists between the types, degrees and durations of stressors on a people and some classic community conditions, violent behaviors and some mental and physical illnesses.

It is increasingly apparent that stress, mental health and violence are linked.

How one reacts to stress in general has much to do with how much or little control a person has over critical areas, such as wherewithal to secure the basic life needs for self and family. Individuals living in affected communities have had limited control as resources have been governed by institutional elements that historically practice unjustified social favoritism and bias. Nor do they have control over the consequent response dynamics such as gangs and the unrelenting "war on gangs", which contributes to their collective stress and frustration experience.

Revisit William, standing in his kitchen as shots burst through the wall ending his brother's life. Imagine for one moment the unimaginable – the horror he witnessed as his brother's life was horrifically minced before his eyes; the sights and sounds of his brother's smiling face suddenly exploding, splattering blood, bone and brains, mixed with his mother's unholy screams as her worst fears are realized. His young mind shuts off in self-defense. Minimally, the trauma of this event has certainly shaped his outlook on life. He now knows from personal experience what millions of children in "reservation communities" have learned in much the same way: how cheap life is and how easily it can be taken away. He would necessarily adopt coping mechanisms set to the most primal common denominator: basic human survival which, as he painfully learned, he has little control over. Living day-to-day, fearful of the violent present there is little room for thoughts of the future. He begins to lose social feeling. He needs to focus on his own survival - others will have to fend for themselves.

His experience is shared by many others in his neighborhood. They have this as their unholy bond rather than camping, sports triumphs or educational achievements. Society says this is "normal" for his people... *"It's cultural, familial, and likely genetic"*. It is society's illogical *justification* that he is forced to accept. Without real understanding there is little hope for the future of his neighborhood, and for the next William. And without serious and informed professional help, the future is uncertain for this William and the too many like him now and for generations to come.

Yours, mine and ours: divorce is not an option

Violence anywhere will always have far reaching consequences. In the last decade of the 20th century, youth violence, like drug abuse, has spread to the once tranquil halls of that *other* America. We have buried white children in Paducah, Kentucky; Springfield, Oregon; Littleton, Colorado, San Diego, California, and where next? These may be new, unusual and still rare but they are here. There remains the *other* world where William and Rebecca, and Carlos and Littlefeather, routinely live and die much too young, mentally, physically and spiritually.

Even if structural societal changes do not occur, mental health research and counseling must be directed at this continuing nightmare some children routinely endure. Increasing numbers of individuals, families and peoples experience psyche altering trauma that makes people sick and engenders reactionary 'black sheep' ready to release built-up and highly charged emotions left undiagnosed and untreated, some over decades and generations.

The results of repeated exposure to horrific physical violence in civilian settings in combination with social, economic and the many forms of sanctioned violence are yet to be linked and evaluated. However, it appears that stress and violence have a deleterious effect on growing numbers of young people. It should also be clear that allowing any kind of violence to exist let alone thrive is unhealthy and escalates the probability of successive and spread violence.

These are critical issues that help determine a person's emotional and physical ability to cope with the rigors of daily routine, the demands of interpersonal relationships as well as clarity and esteem required for future goal setting and accomplishment.

17

A Violence Beyond Gangs

Throughout this book we discuss the many kinds of violence, its many paths, consequences and outcomes. Societal violence appears to be motivated by self-interests and deep-seated beliefs in racial superiority. The uneven management of resources and the power and wealth generated is part of that motivation. Societal violence does harm to the targeted individual, family, community and group in a physical, psychological and social sense. These can be active or passive or do harm simply by the act of withholding. Gang violence is an area where motivations appear to be confusing if not illogical. Certainly there is reason that can be applied to this devastating phenomenon.

The foundational gang type is the **Traditional Gang**, this is the same-race and same-group gang that primarily kills their own. There are other deviant activities within these groups but the foundation of American gangs is this one. They use convenient stand-in excuses to remain in an endless state of war against their brethren.

This turning against one's own group is a manifestation of antipathy turned self-hatred and hopelessness for their group's existence and standing. They view their group as a societal failure. They have framed their *mirror image* as the cause of their overwhelming anger, rage and at fault for collective failure…they *deserve* to die.

An elaborate ruse has thus been devised to vanquish their "enemy" using symbols (colors, turf, etc.) as legitimate reasons to engage in what is in effect, a slow process of self-elimination. They have reached a point of psychopathology.

Law enforcement experts and renowned researchers classify this violent gang behavior as being over *turf, status and revenge* and build on this paradigm for prevention and punishment. Research chooses to accept this aberrant paradigm rather than delve beneath the obvious. Let us summarize a broader picture...

An important consideration in our analysis of violence is *how* and *why* such a pathological road had been devised and why so many youth, male and female, take it.

Basic needs for survival

An individual has to be able to satisfy a set of needs in order to survive and to function more or less normally. Abraham Maslow observed that there are five sets of human goals arranged in hierarchies with each succeeding level relying on the prior need upon which to build. Four of these are the most basic needs for survival and normalcy: physiological, safety/security, love/belongingness and esteem. The fifth is self-actualization. This simply means that a body will satisfy hunger, thirst and other basic needs *before* pondering the meaning of life, playing a game of tennis or visiting an art gallery. Moreover, we are motivated by the desire to secure and maintain the various conditions upon which these most basic human needs rest. Maslow calls these the *deficiency needs* or *D-needs*.

Maslow stated, *"Any thwarting or possibility of thwarting of these basic human goals, or danger to the defenses which protect them, or to the conditions upon which they rest, is considered to be a psychological threat. With a few exceptions, all psychopathology may be partially traced to such threats. It is such basic threats which bring about the general emergency reactions."* (Maslow, 1943)

The point is that if basic needs are threatened the body goes into survival mode: *remove the threat to basic needs or face death.* And translated to the upside-down and confused street milieu where perceived threats are *made* real: *kill the motha fucka.* Should needs remain unmet and/or deficient, such pathological condition is likely to emerge along with other deviant behaviors and/or illnesses.

This coincides with research by Dr. Karina Walters, Madeline Drexler, Dr. Maria Yellow Horse Brave Heart, Dr. Hans Selve, Kruk, Meelis, Halarz, Haller and others cited in earlier chapters whereby the added intense exposure to extraordinary traumas and stressors can cause profound damage to the psyche, the body, soul and spirit. And such damage can carry forward through generations. The body cannot remain under such stresses or becomes vulnerable to Post Traumatic Stress Disorder, Attention Deficit Disorder, Anxiety, Depression, Shock and Panic Disorder, self-destructive acts and thoughts of suicide and related lethal behaviors. In addition, other research cited here illustrates that the unrelenting *unjustified* nature of the ill-treatment provokes frustration, anger and rage build-up to potential psychopathologies and related negative outcomes. **Such major damage has been done to the collective body in "reservation communities".** This is what should be meant by the term, "at-risk youth".

➤ Institutional policies and practices that practice and affirm dehumanization, marginalization, exploitation, deprivation and directed violence up to and including attempted annihilation do all of these and thwart or otherwise do harm to a group's basic and significant needs which greatly increases potential for negative outcomes.

➤ The types, severity and duration of such deviant *societal* behaviors will have impact on the type, severity and duration of negative reactive and release behaviors (outcomes).

In other words, there is a relationship of (societal) cause and ("reservation community") effect.

The "reservation community" is a pathological deviation from the norm. Its existence is an anomaly. It evolved over decades and generations of groups being subjected to extreme harm and extraordinarily destructive acts and conditions. Thus we are overwhelmed by elevated numbers of "reservation" youth doing themselves and each other in, seemingly automatically. Any society that impairs groups in this manner can expect such a 'return on investment'.

As the entire process begins and institutionalizes, it has an increasing multiplier effect among the affected populace.

Negative social modifications evolve in place of otherwise socially productive patterns, specially as relates to economic and social pursuits. One manifestation of this aspect is another type of gang and activity, the **Predator Gangs,** "mafias that deal in drugs, personal belongings and other 'commodities'. Over time, the "reservation community" child is increasingly at risk of behaving within this abnormal environment in increasingly deviant ways. The abnormal ecology encourages abnormal behaviors that become so prevalent as to seem "normal".

If we understand the dynamics involved then we can no longer accept the ill person's explanation for his acting out, e.g., "He disrespected me"; "I'm defending my 'hood, man"; "I'll die for my homies and "soldado por vida"; and, "That's just the way it is, man".

He sees his situation in desperate and even absolute terms of protecting physical and/or emotional basic needs but in an upside-down reality. And he will go to his death and kill others over this pathological belief structure.

This is not to suggest that everyone in the communities we are concerned with is ill, but they certainly are extraordinarily stressed in critical areas of daily life which can weaken the person spiritually, emotionally and physically and lead to illness. Additionally, structural deficiencies negatively impact esteem, self-actualization and success.

18

Social Ecology:
nurturing or debilitating?

Laws, regulations and social policy favoring the majority group have been in use since before the birth of this nation. Children born into this group find for the most part nurturing, acceptance, empathy, cohesion, significantly better education, social acceptance and cultural reinforcement. Consequently, these persons enjoy increased probability of remaining healthy and developing their potential and becoming contributing members of their community and of society.

Groups clustered onto "reservation communities" are born into a less healthy environment where basic needs are met with greater difficulty. Their children emerge into a world of societal alienation, violent and destructive sub-cycles, discouragement and hopelessness.

The discovery of the epigenome explains how it is possible for members of succeeding generations to "inherit" earlier cumulative trauma as well as having to deal with contemporary events. The emotional and psychological resources available to a child to deal with such adverse stressors are for the most part inadequate. Hence, their ability to fully develop their potential is limited.

Many members in the community are functionally illiterate. This outcome is a form of violence that could have been corrected long ago. The "reservation" child lives in the same world that we all do. He sees the vast differences in communities and ways of life. The child's increasing low self-esteem and feelings of hopelessness are not just signs of damaged emotional health and well being but reflects a realistic assessment of his chances and opportunities. And portends future failure for him and his group…and he knows it.

Despite deficient resources children in these environments do well to mitigate effects upon them. Even under stressful conditions, most of these children learn all that is presented to them and more; some turn to athletics; some go to work but a few turn to gangs to "succeed". And like a disease, their presence is felt way beyond their numbers. Regardless of the strategy chosen, the row they have to hoe is a much more difficult one.

Youth that emerge successfully are said to have "overcome adversity". *But the adversity is artificially created and maintained by the very society that claims to want to "solve" the violence problem.* Rather, society accepts and promotes that the community has mysteriously but somehow *inherently* become a "war zone" requiring declarations of war.

Their group has been violated. Their rights and freedoms, their opportunities and potential, their health and environment, their educational attainment, their hopes and dreams have all suffered major body blows. **Substantial violence has already been done to the "reservation community" before its members react in violence.**

An act of violence regardless of source or type impacts the victim's sphere of influence, i.e. family, friends and community. As violence increases in an area, violence affected spheres overlap and permeate the environment until seemingly everyone living there has been touched by violence in some way, and almost every home has a tragic tale to tell. The community is left without defenses and children are pretty much on their own to deal with all of it. To the extent that a society does not help its children meet their basic needs and fails to correct inadequacies repeatedly and over generations, that society can expect that increasing numbers of

166

these children will engage in negative behaviors which the society will have to tend.

When authorities say we have to "give up on this generation…" parents eventually come to believe this lie about their babies. Causes and triggering dynamics remain misdiagnosed and the now dependent "reservation community" seems ready to give up its youth to authorities. The extent of all of this damage is not nearly understood, appreciated and therefore dealt with in ways that would change the process to violent outcomes.

The popular view of youth violence being *cyclical* and related to genetics, culture and family and peer ties extends to so-called cycles of: *welfare, substance abuse, family abuse, family breakdown, unemployment, school failure, etc.* These are all *cycles of violence* but are also *outcomes* of the same societal process that produces multi-generational gangs.

Common habits and ways of life are examined rather than extreme negative causative elements in-common. We employ ways to measure a child's ability to deal with a make-believe reality, a "norm" that applies to another child in another place. These are the "risk" and "protective factors" in and around the child's immediate environment. This model assumes that the problem and the solution are located within the child's ability to correct, and/or his family and peers. They are not and never were.

There is no demonstrated appreciation for the severity and the kinds of violence experiences, both overt and covert, or any understanding of the true sources of violence that are beyond these domains that are having profound effects on the child since before his birth. Professionals simply look at who is aggressive, angry and violent and from that posit that the cause and solution lie within the child and his immediate spheres of influence. In fact, the totality of damage is deep and far reaching and impacts the most fundamental aspects of his being. His learning and future employment are structural casualties but, like gangs are accepted as normal for the group.

Meanwhile, science seeks to prove that biology and culture are somehow related to aggressive behaviors, thus the unrelenting search for genetic and other predisposing factors. This approach may seem like progress but is it? Research may be better served looking beyond the *outcomes* and into possible *causes* and related *evolutions*. The American experience is not a one size fits all. Applying one group's set of experiences to other groups is unrealistic and even dangerous. This allows the mayhem to continue while taking children through a guilt maze that at the end of the day still says loud and clear, *"Do you see all of this heartache, trouble and expense? This is all your people's doing"*.

Black sheep and White sheep

Incidents such as Columbine catch us off-guard in more ways than one. Yes, they brutally remind us of the frailty of human life. But they also illustrate how we as a nation have come to subconsciously accept youth violence among some groups as "normal" while being stunned out of our socks by others. This was made evident by the enormity of national outrage and shock, quickly followed by positive action that was astounding in its breadth and scope when the Columbine innocents were gunned down in gang fashion. All at once the entire nation was focused on the horror of youth violence and ready to invest whatever it takes to end it, there anyway. As these difficult days passed, the entire nation formed an ocean of compassion and flowing resources to the extent that the nation's double standard became painfully obvious.

The President of the United States, the First Lady, the vice-president, major media networks, it seemed the whole world rushed to shore up this community. President Clinton declared "We do not accept this. We will move heaven and earth to prevent it from occurring again." The decision to arrest it in its tracks was made. The children and families were immediately cradled in the country's arms and assured that everything would be OK. For them, America's Safety Net was forming, as strong as steel and as soft as a mother's breast.

Meanwhile, back on America's "reservation communities", millions of beautiful children of color struggle to cope with the knowledge that America plans no such safety net for them. The silence over their traumatic existence is deafening.

It was pointed out that dozens of minority children are gunned down every week, year in and year out and for decades in the schools, parks, on the streets and even in the homes of some neighborhoods throughout this nation, with hardly a nod from leaders and local media. These communities hold neighborhood car washes and bake sales to help defray burial expenses. And mothers of previous murder victims sell their homemade foods to replenish their burial kitty that will assist other mothers, names yet unknown, to bury their to-be murdered children. These communities have adjusted to the unnatural reality of their children dying at the hands of other children over time and for the long haul and with no end in sight. Discussions of when and where it began are not entered in to. Only that it got that way a long time ago and we can't seem to stop it. We give ridiculous explanation for it with justifying rationalizations (Stanly "Tookie" Williams starting the Crips).

Columbine-like incidents developed over time albeit much shorter, and no one saw them coming. However, there will be no oversimplified explanations here such as Eric Harris and Dylan Klebold being credited with initiating "White School Shootings" or "White Group Murder" nor will such incidents ever be accepted as a *cycle of (white) violence.* Each and every incident affecting the majority population is guaranteed to be analyzed and solved if it takes going back to Adam and Eve.

All at once, white America experienced the horror and sadness that only the untimely and violent death of a child can generate. However, the response for each America was and is very different. And unless one looks at the entire picture objectively they miss the differences. One is a military response and the other an army of friendly resources.

Now revisit San Diego, Paducah, Springfield and even Littleton, Colorado - and next maybe your community? What would happen if childhood murders were accepted as "normal for your kind" and allowed to be a daily event with hardly a nod elsewhere? And how would their children fare in their own lifetimes and over generations?

Columbine-type attacks will be slowed if not stopped due to the massive efforts directed at *this* youth violence. Still, trauma from related kinds of violence will affect white families in other ways. Children are into gangs and hate is constantly being promoted so violence volatility remains high.

International terrorism brings home similar feelings of helplessness and vulnerability but not nearly on the constant scale as in barrios and ghettos. Those in our Armed Forces are feeling the effects of a similar kind of war much as these children do. They will show the same signs of trauma and stress related illness. These feelings may be new to mainstream America but are usual to her "reservation" children. If it hits your family or community, welcome to my world.

America will continue to invest friendly resources in safety nets for the Columbines of the one world. But unless we stop the causes of youth violence everywhere there will be more of them. Trying to maintain two different worlds in one orbit is not really possible and the effort takes extraordinary time and resources and yet, we keep trying. For children in our "reservation communities", our response continues to be police gang units, jails and prisons, welfare offices, unemployment centers and so on. These will never stop the carnage.

America's minority groups live with violence everyday and they know the death of their children will not bring a President to declare an emergency or a call to action. There will be no official cries for safety nets heard here, only of slamming prison doors and the silent wringing of hands.

Any critical analysis of American history cannot escape concluding America is a land of two societies: one with the American Dream intact, the other living a daily nightmare; one a teeming river and the other a crimson flow. America's separate and unequal track record reflects an unconscionable waste of youthful humanity.

We must understand that violence goes both ways and violence, regardless of form will always beget violence. Some of the violent results are visible and some are not, as they are internalized and absorbed deeply within the individual and the community. The societal systems are the problem and the solution. To rely on the justice system for solution to community violence is to continue to have no solution.

As a sad consequence of social misdeeds and miscalculations, the tragic reality is that there are youth that live almost everywhere ready to kill and be killed. Yes, they must be removed from society. However, even in the most severely impacted areas, it is well known by law enforcement that fewer than five-percent of a youth population can be considered gang involved and fewer are hard-core. Strangely, over decades and generations this dynamic never sways. Is it a DNA issue? A parenting issue? A media issue? Seems a small enough number to analyze and correct, if we wanted to.   *

Gangs are a national phenomenon…but must be solved locally.

In these communities, as Albert Bandura has rightly pointed out, we must take into account how *personal, environmental* and *behavioral* factors interact. Moreover, any solution that is proposed must address these areas. It is not enough to deal with the personal conflicts of the violent person without reference to his environment. There are also unseen environmental factors that contribute to the conditions that make for violence. (Bandura, 1999) These include the institutional policies, acts and practices both inside and outside a community that affect persons within the community. Solutions must involve the youth of course, but also political, business and social leaders, residents, law enforcement and the judicial system as *solutions exists among all of these domains as well.*

We are engaged in a constant tug of war among different groups of Americans. What is only now beginning to become clear is that the problem of youth violence can touch any community. Youth violence is but one form of violence that emerges where people are structurally marginalized and dehumanized within a social system, but its spread to other parts of the system will inevitably occur in some form or fashion. Accepting and promoting inclusion and equality rather than fighting to the death over them is prerequisite to combating youth and other forms of community violence. Understanding this conflictive and uneasy social maladjustment is only important if we wish to foster group inclusion - a process that should be, after all, the story of America.

End of Volume 1

For additional information, charts and diagrams, please refer to New Paradigms Group, *Forces…Gangs to Riots Series, "The Peace and Violence Continuum"*, Part 1 and Part 2.

*

Volume 2 covers the gang experience, the gang cocoon, the gang Prime Directive, the three and only kinds of street gangs: Self-Hate (same-group), Hate (other groups) and Predator (mafias), their motivations and more that might help you to get a grip on this national problem manifesting in your community.

For additional information, charts and diagrams, please refer to New Paradigms Group, *Forces…Gangs to Riots Series, "The Peace and Violence Continuum"*, Part 2 and Part 3.

*

Volume 3 outlines the analytics of violence and peace in an evolutionary process in detailed charts, diagrams and with explanations. This is an education and training track for communities deciding to systemically end their gang problem.

For additional information, charts and diagrams, please refer to New Paradigms Group, *Forces…Gangs to Riots Series, "The Peace and Violence Continuum"*, Parts 1-4.

About the author

On a recent trip to LA, my friend Leo Cortez drove me through the same streets we both worked then and he still does. They were gone…the men were gone! An entire generation wiped out! Why? And what is next for these children, the families and these neighborhoods?

I remember back to my first days as a youth counselor, cringing at the official explanations for young people killing each other…and are still told today: "They're born that way; it's in their genes", "It's part of their culture", "They learn it from their elders", "It's territorial…like an animal peeing on trees and then they will kill to defend it", it's the "The Hatfields and McCoys", and "They have a blood lust because they descended from African tribes and Aztecs who cannibalized and sacrificed their own". The reasoning goes round and round in training and in books with the same deviant themes embedded in racial, cultural and familial peculiarities. These have become accepted as causes of endless cycles of violence. Some explanations are more elaborate than others, but the premise is the same: ***it's all their own doing.***

It reminded me of when as a young man I had the opportunity to volunteer with young people from the San Fernando Valley and really enjoyed it. But my career was headed toward business and real estate. In 1971, I agreed to take a short six-month break to assist my friend Ray Otero to rebuild a community center that had been a community anchor since 1928, located in the heart of East Los Angeles. It was then that I was introduced to the gangs – an introduction that would last a lifetime.

I found the gang world bone-chilling and impossible to understand - that children could murder children and all around were resigned to it. I still do not know what made me change course but I spent the next twenty-five years deeply involved in trying to end it. It was tough and I wanted to retreat many times. However, I as well as many others couldn't and wouldn't accept failure in this seemingly no-brainer quest to stop youthful murder.

We were always outnumbered and short on resources. We tried almost in vain to stop the waste and carnage, rushing back and forth giving everything we had to stem the crimson flow. I was one with many other peace warriors, not knowing why, ready to do and some of us died.

I worked hard and fought harder in the mindless struggle disguised as a war against gangs. I witnessed acts unheard of in a modern society, yet not worthy of the news of the day. I witnessed the gang wars, the funerals and the riots. I saw parents' anguish, their unfathomable grief and losses of innocence multiplied a thousand-fold where there should have been happy childhoods and families. I died a little each time a senseless act claimed another predestined victim. And as everyone else involved, I had no time to think, only to react.

I'm not a cop or a banger but got to know both sides well, better than they knew each other. I count among my acquaintances dealers and prosecutors, cops and killers. I was respected in both camps. But as happens in this upside down world, I was sometimes targeted by errant members of both factions. It was a strange world of action-reaction mixed with mayhem and confusion.

For the last ten years of my career, I served as head of the nation's then largest anti-gang agency, a killer job that should not need to exist. And I survived, sort of. Many did not.

I finally retreated from that world of dread, thankful to be alive, not immediately realizing the full toll to be paid. I may never be the same but know I am one of the lucky ones. For once the maelstrom of youth violence lands, it shows no mercy and plays no favorites.

In the process I learned something. I found a thread to other threads that connect the dots to what is officially a mystery of the age - a mystery that destroys our peace and shakes our complacency - a mystery that brutally but finally grabs your attention when you bury your dead. I wish to pass on this information in the interest of maybe saving the life of a future president of this great nation, or maybe more important, the father or mother of an intact family. And so others wanting to help may learn from my experiences, both good and bad. I learned the subject well...got it firsthand. As you read on you will come to understand what I came to realize: that there is no mystery at all. There is a method to this madness and logic to the puzzle of youth violence.

One year after agreeing to the six-month stint to help rebuild the Cleland House Community Center, I was appointed its executive director. I was 23. I was learning about gangs and the madness surrounding them while planning the new center out of one of the few dilapidated buildings left standing.

Just outside, drugs and violence ruled this world while inside were children and families. Out of the barrios, a few bold local leaders emerged led by Leo Cortez. These young men were making peace among themselves and other gang neighborhoods. The Cleland House would serve as the support and host for their efforts. It was dangerous, but working alongside some truly dedicated people, peace was established in one of the toughest and deadliest gang areas of Los Angeles and at that time, the country.

Leo and Margaret Cortez were instrumental throughout. Leo organized and headed the *Federation de Barrios Unidos,* the volunteer group of gang leadership working as peace ambassadors to negotiate volatile issues to peaceful resolution and to quell disturbances before they got out of hand. Leo's Federation was the gang intervention and organizing element. Cleland House or what was left of it was where prevention, intervention and community mobilization programs emanated. This became the model for creating peace in a gang community.

Leo and the ambassadors hammered out peace agreements among the barrios…and those years saw the lowest rate of gang homicides in decades. Later they would select young fathers from the local gangs to work on the construction of the new community center. Margaret organized the mothers and youth in community improvement activities and fund raisers.

The place was buzzing "like in the old days". Our success attracted attention and with the help and investment of many but especially one Francis Breen of the Max C. Fleischmann Foundation, we built the new community center with day care, counseling/tutoring rooms, pool, gym and more. And with it a great measure of pride was injected into a community.

This was the first time a state of the art community center was built sans government help but with local fund raisers and private donations. The new center opened its doors in 1983 to the entire community and for years was not marked by graffiti or warfare.

Then in 1983 I was asked to lead Los Angeles' Community Youth Gang Service (CYGS) project, a gang intervention operation whose design was based on the Federation concept. Our "target area" was now Los Angeles. It stretched from Compton to the San Fernando Valley and from Santa Monica to the San Gabriel Valley. Our group and many others were in the thick of it during the most tumultuous period in gang violence history. I was given a crash course in the politics of gangs and of gang programs.

CYGS was restricted to employing ex-gang members to quell gang disturbances but without the prevention, community mobilization or resources. I worked desperately to expand the strategy while cleaning up a program in disrepute (LA Times Metro 2/14/93).

We surreptitiously secured funding for prevention, education, employment, mobilization and other activities but for a very few areas. And again gang activity markedly subsided as verified by the Los Angeles Police and Sheriff's Department and the Los Angeles City Office of Criminal Justice Planning. We managed to help organize communities while installing programs in schools and communities such as Career Paths, Star-Kids, and A Season of Peace (Thanksgiving to New Year peace treaties – a foothold that could be extended and worked from).

We never did get the resources or the "OK" to do the job right. In fact, the opposite was true. Comprehensive efforts were heavily discouraged to the point funds were withdrawn rather than used for holistic services.

It was during this time that my good friend, then Probation Officer Gene Anderson and I formalized this Target Area Strategy (TAS), the cornerstone that still stands as the best and most effective method for a community to combat gangs - the same approach that brought peace to the Cleland House area of East Los Angeles.

The Target Area Strategy (TAS) was subsequently adopted by the greater Los Angeles Inter-Agency Gang Task Force and served as a national model. The first ever major change in gang work was underway. The plan was used to train the Los Angeles Sheriff Department, the LAPD and more than 85 community agencies. This was the first time anywhere that an integrated, multi-agency gang abatement plan required inter-agency coordination and collaboration. The strategy required agencies to work together under one lead agency to minimize administrative overhead thus better serve a target area. This "consortium model" was also adopted as a national model.

The TAS first educated a local target area "team" about the types and gradations of gangs and activity. Agreement was reached about which services were appropriate to address particular situations. Monitoring tools would measure the effectiveness of each targeting plan. The strategy required participation by an area's local businesses, schools, churches, parents, community groups and law enforcement under one coordinating umbrella. We as an agency were prevented by funding mandate from doing this ourselves but assisted target

176

area teams to implement their integrated plan as consortia. This strategy continues to be the recommended method for combating gang violence. In 1993, my efforts were acknowledged in the *Congressional Record.*

At the height of my career I questioned my own 25 year involvement in the quest to end gang violence. I knew that something was missing. The other experts I had heard were not hitting it…I was not hitting it.

While for years many of us knew gang violence was self-destructive, in 1993 I publicly expressed a different way of viewing such violence: *"gang violence is hate violence…self-hate violence" (L.A. Times 2/19/1993).*

At the time, that news article announced my exit from gang work. However, it also marked the beginning of this book.

We had made significant contributions to the work and to communities experiencing gang activity that are a matter of public record, including combining corporate funds with local dollars to build a community center; then revolutionizing gang work by developing the first cross-disciplined target area strategy that assessed gang influence in specific areas and combining prevention, education, mobilization and intervention strategies via agency consortia to maximize resources and for accountability. Although we pioneered these in the 70's and 80's, these core strategies remain today.

I left the work a tired and humbled man, knowing that while some efforts saved lives and changed how the battle against gangs was fought, I knew instinctively the wrong battle was being waged. I am dedicating time and energy to help wage a new battle and hopefully a more productive one.

Steven

I have known Steven for over 30 years. I had first heard of the important work Steven had done in building Cleland House in East Los Angeles. Together with local residents they organized a community where several gangs had been at war for decades and accomplished the rebuilding of a multi-service community center that had burned to the ground during the tumultuous 1960's. They recruited persons from different gangs to work on the project, earning the center the reputation as a neutral location where making peace became one of their most important and successful programs. The center became a showcase of community self-determination combined with business logic. Steve was always known for being able to tackle the most difficult jobs, and working gangs in Los Angeles in the 1970's and 80's was among the toughest of jobs. So in 1983, when he was recruited to head LA's Community Youth Gang Service project (CYGS), he took on one of the most difficult tasks in the country. Steve became a nationally recognized expert on gangs, but not on purpose. When he spoke, he hardly mentioned colors or turf. He talked of history and aspirations and families broken and dreams unrealized. He told of children and mothers experiencing a world that few understood. He spoke of generations of failure for all of us. But when he was done, you understood the gang problem. He did a great job as Executive Director of that agency and his Target Area Strategy remains the underpinning of gang intervention work in the nation. I was privileged to have served as Chairman of the Board of Directors of CYGS. Here we bring together psychology, culture and learning so as to begin a dialog aimed at preventing and treating the root causes of community violence. This book will be useful for schoolteachers and parents, counselors, therapists, religious leaders, police officers and policy makers - not to replace the work they are doing, but to provide valuable insight leading to greater effectiveness in their endeavors. It is hoped this is the beginning of a dialog and actions that will connect us in more human ways to all of our children. For those that are connected to others through their humanity cannot kill their neighbors.

Fernando Hernandez, PhD

Selected Bibliography

Wiley, Steven R. 1997. Violent Street Gangs in America. *Violent Street Gangs in America*, Testimony before US Senate, April 23. http://www.hi-ho.ne.jp/taku77/refer/gang.htm.

US Bureau of Justice Statistics. 2010. Bureau of Justice Statistics (BJS) - Total correctional population. US Bureau of Justice Statistics. *Bureau of Justice Statistics*. March 9. http://bjs.ojp.usdoj.gov/index.cfm?ty=tp&tid=11.

Anderson, C. A., L. Berkowitz, E. Donnerstein, L. R. Huesmann, J. D. Johnson, D. Linz, N. M. Malamuth, and E. Wartella. 2003. The influence of media violence on youth. *Psychological Science in the Public Interest* 4, no. 3: 81-110.

Crutchfield, R. D., and T. Wadsworth. 2003. Poverty and Violence. *International Handbook of Violence Research*: 67.

Howell, J. C., and A. Egley. 2005. Gangs in small towns and rural counties. *NYGC Bulletin* 1.

Kean, T. H., L. H. Hamilton, R. Ben-Veniste, B. Kerrey, F. F. Fielding, J. F. Lehman, J. S. Gorelick, T. J. Roemer, S.

Gorton, and J. R. Thompson. 2004. *The 9/11 commission report*. Storming Media.

Graves, Joseph. 2004. *The Race Myth*. 1st ed. Dutton Adult.

Blatt, Jessica. 2007. Scientific Racism. In *The Blackwell Encyclopedia of Sociology*, ed. Ritzer. Oxford, UK, Malden, USA and Carlton, Australia: Blackwell Publishing Ltd. http://www.sociologyencyclopedia.com.mimas.calstatela.edu/subscriber/uid=1939/tocnode?g9781405124331_chunk_g978140512433125_ss1-54>

Raper, A. F. 2003. *The tragedy of lynching*. Dover Pubns.

Tolnay, S. E., and E. M. Beck. 1995. *A festival of violence: An analysis of southern lynchings, 1882-1930*. Univ of Illinois Pr.

NPR. 2007. NPR: Atlanta Considers Saggy Pants Ban. *NPR News & Views*. August 23. http://www.npr.org/blogs/newsandviews/2007/08/atlanta_considers_saggy_pants_1.html.

Stolberg, Sheryl. 1993. Fear Clouds Search for Genetic Roots of Violence : Sociology: Many say studies could open the door to abuses and racism. Scientists are sharply divided. *Los Angeles Times*. December 30. http://articles.latimes.com/1993-12-30/news/mn-6875_1_genetic-studies.

Peck, D. The Atlantic, How a New Jobless Era Will Transform America http://www.theatlantic.com/doc/201003/jobless-america-future

Spencer, M., Dupree, D., Hartmann, T.; A Phenomenological Variant of Ecological Systems Theory (PVEST): A self-organizational perspective in context

Wilson, J., Kelling, G., "Broken Windows", Atlantic Monthly, March 1982 http://en.wikipedia.org/wiki/Fixing_Broken_Windows

Bandura, A. (1994) "Self-Efficacy" http://www.des.emory.edu/mfp/BanEncy.html

The Register; Lettice, J., (2005) http://www.theregister.co.uk/2005/01/13/genewatch_dna_database/

Levine, H.G. Gettman, J. B., Reirnarman, C., Small, D.P (2010) Drug Arrests and DNA: Building Jim Crow's Database: http://dragon.soc.qc.cuny.edu/Staff/levine/Drug-Arrests-and-DNA-Abstract-from-GeneWatch_Vol21No3-4.pdf

ABC News, (2007), *This Week with George Stephanopoulos*, Interview with Treasury Secretary Henry Paulson, March 4, 2007.

Asian Nation, Construction and Destruction, http://www.asian-nation.org/internment.shtml, retrieved August 30, 2007.

Bandura, A. (1986) *Social Foundations of Thought and Action, : A social cognitive theory*, Prentice-Hall (Englewood Cliffs, N.J.

Bandura, A. (1994). Self-efficacy. In V. S. Ramachaudran (Ed.), Encyclopedia of human behavior (Vol. 4, pp. 71-81). New York: Academic Press. (Reprinted in H. Friedman [Ed.], Encyclopedia of mental health. San Diego: Academic Press, 1998)

Becker, A., Randels, J., Theodore, D.Engaging Youth as Agents of Change in a Youth Violence Prevention Project, *Community Youth Development Journal* http://www.cydjournal.org/2005Fall/contents.html

Becker, M.G., Hall, J.S., Ursic, C.M., Jain, S. and Calhoun, D. (2004). Caught in the cross-fire: The effects of a peer-based intervention program for violently injured youth. Journal of Adolescent Health, 34:177-183.

Camino, L. and Zeldin, S. (2002). From Periphery to Center: Pathways for Youth Civic Engagement in the Day-to-Day Lives of communities. Applied Developmental Science, 6 (4), 213-220.

Carnegie Council on Adolescent Development (1992). A matter of time: Risk and opportunities in the nonschool hours. Recommendations for strengthening community programs for youth. Washington, D.C.: Author.

Carroll, G.B., Hébert, D.M.C., and Roy, J.M. (1999).Youth action strategies in violence prevention. Journal of Adolescent Health, 25:7-13.

Centers for Disease Control and Prevention, National Center for Injury Prevention and Control. *Youth Violence: Fact Sheet*, 03/10/06 http://www.cdc.gov/ncipc/factsheets/yvfacts.htm

Children Now, A Different World, Children's Perceptions of Race and Class in the Media,**http://publications.childrennow.org-/assets/pdf/cmp/diffworld99/assets/pdf/cmp/diffworld99/diff-world-99-v1.pdf**

CNN.com, (2005), Bennett Underfire for Remarks on Blacks, Crime, September 30, 2005,http://www.cnn.com/2005/POLITICS-/09/30/bennett.comments/,retrieved September 31, 2005.

Cummings, S., and D. J. Monti. 1993. *Gangs: The origins and impact of contemporary youth gangs in the United States*. State Univ of New York Pr.

Department Of The Navy - Naval Historical Center, Navajo Code Talkers: World War II Fact Sheet; www.history.navy.mil/faqs/faq61-2.htm, retrieved September 3, 2007

Dr. Kevin Franklin, Ed.D. Executive Director; Center for Computing in the Humanities, Arts and Social Sciences; Senior Research Scientist, National Center for Supercomputing Applications, University of Illinois at Urbana Champaign

Eccles, J. and Gootman, J.A. (Eds.) (2002). Community Programs to Promote Youth Development. Wash., DC: National Academies Press.

Egley Jr, A., and C. E Ritz. 2006. Highlights of the 2004 National Youth Gang Survey. *OJJDP Fact Sheet*.

English,T.J.(1991)Westies,St. Martin's Press, New York, New York.

Fried, A. (1993) *The Rise and Fall of the Jewish Gangster in America,* New York, New York, Columbia University Press.

Gonzales-Day, K. 2006. *Lynching in the West, 1850-1935*. Duke Univ Press

180

Gover, K. (2000) Remarks Of Kevin Gover, Assistant Secretary-Indian *Affairs: Address To Tribal Leaders,* Friday, September 8th, 2000 on the Occasion of the Ceremony Acknowledging the 175th Anniversary of the Establishment of the Bureau of Indian Affairs (Washington, DC), Journal of American Indian Education, Volume 39 Number 2 Winter 2000, Special Issue 3.

Howell,J., Egley, A., Gleason, D., Modern-Day Youth Gangs, Juvenile Justice Bulletin, (2002), Office of Juvenile Justice and Delinquency Prevention, Washington DC.

Knox, L., Bacho, A., Hahn, G and others. Youth as Change Agents in Distressed Immigrant Communities, *Community Youth Development Journal,*http://www.cyd-journal.org/2005Fall/contents.html.

Le, C.N. , 2007. "Construction and Destruction: Japanese American Internment" Asian-Nation: The Landscape of Asian America, http://www.asian-nation.org/internment.shtml, retrieved 09/3/2007

Luthar, S. S., & Zigler, E. (1991). Vulnerability and competence: A review of research on resilience in childhood. American Journal of Orthopsychiatry, 61, 6-19.

Maxson, C. L. 1998. *Gang Members on the Move.* Bulletin. Youth Gang Series. Washington, DC: U.S. Department of Justice, Office of Juvenile Justice and Delinquency Prevention. (Adobe PDF)

Mercy J A, Rosenberg M L , Powel K E, Broome C V , and Roper W L (1993). Public Health Policy for Preventing Violence, Health Affairs, Vol 12, Issue 4, 7-29

Miller, W. (2001). The Growth of Youth Gang Problems in the United States: 1970–98, Washington, DC: U.S. Department of Justice, Office of Justice Programs, OJJDP.

Moyers, Bill. Bill Moyers Journal . James H. Cone | PBS. *Bill Moyers Journal.* http://www.pbs.org/moyers/journal/11232007/profile.html.

National Japanese American Historical Society, *Research on 100/442nd Regimental Combat Team,*http://www.nikkeiheritage.org/research/442.html

National Youth Gang Center (2000). *1998 National Youth Gang Survey.* Washington, DC: U.S. Department of Justice, Office of Justice Programs, Office of Juvenile Justice and Delinquency Prevention.

National Youth Gang Center. 1997. *National Youth Gang Center. 1997. 1995 National Youth Gang Survey. Washington, DC: U.S. Department of Justice, Office of Justice Programs, Office of Juvenile Justice and Delinquency Prevention..* Washington, DC: U.S. Department of Justice, Office of Justice Programs, Office of Juvenile Justice and Delinquency Prevention.

National Youth Gang Center. 1999a. *1996 National Youth Gang Survey.* Washington, DC: U.S. Department of Justice, Office of Justice Programs, Office of Juvenile Justice and Delinquency Prevention, July 1999.

National Youth Gang Center. 1999b. *1997 National Youth Gang Survey.* Washington, DC: U.S. Department of Justice, Office of Justice Programs, OJJDP, December 1999.

National Youth Gang Center. *Frequently Asked Questions Regarding Gangs.* Institute for Intergovernmental Research, Washington, DC: U.S. Department of Justice, Office of Justice Programs, Office of Juvenile Justice and Delinquency Prevention. Retrieved March, 10, 2005, from http://www.iir.com/nygc/faq.htm

Reppetto, T.A. (2004) American Mafia : A history of its rise to power / Thomas Reppetto Published New York : H. Holt, 1st ed.

Skinner, B.F. (1971), *Beyond freedom and dignity.* New York: Knopf.

Snoop Dogg, Tha Eastsidaz - Another Day, from Snoop Dogg Presents The Eastsidaz, Doggystyle Records, 2000

Starbuck, D., Howell, J. C., and Lindquist, D. J. 2001. *Hybrid and Other Modern Gangs*. Bulletin. Youth Gang Series. Washington, DC: U.S. Department of Justice, OJJDP

American Academy of Pediatrics, Task Force on Violence (1999). The Role of the Pediatrician In Youth Violence Prevention in Clinical Practice and at the Community Level, *Pediatrics*;103;173-181, American Academy of Pediatrics, 141 Northwest Point Boulevard, Elk Grove Village, Illinois, 60007

The National Archives, December 1982, Retrieved 09/2007 www.archives.gov/research/japanese-americans/justice-denied/

U.S. Department of Health and Human Services, 2001. *Youth Violence: A Report of the Surgeon General*, Retrieved from http://www.surgeongeneral.gov/library/youthviolence/ March 10, 2006

U.S. Public Health Service, (2001), A *Report of the Surgeon General on Youth Violence*,

Washington, DC: Department of Health and Human Services, http://www.surgeongeneral.gov/library/youthviolence/toc.html, retrieved on January 7, 2006)

Ungar, S.J. (1995) Fresh blood : the new American immigrants, New York :Simon & Schuster.

United States Senate (03/23/1997) Violent Street Gangs in America, Statement of Steven R. Wiley, Chief Violent Crimes and Major Offenders Section, Federal Bureau of Investigation, Before the Senate Committee on the Judiciary, United States Senate, *Washington, D.C.*

Wikipedia, Ira Hayes, (http://en.wikipedia.org/wiki/Ira_Hayes, retrieved September 3, 2007).

Witt, Howard. 2005. Old South racism lives in Texas town - chicagotribune.com. *Chicago Tribune e-Edition.* June 5. http://www.chicagotribune.com/services/newspaper/eedition/chi-050605johnsonbeating-story,0,4577534,full.story.

World Health Organization / European Commission: *"Balancing mental health promotion and mental health care: a joint World Health Organization / European Commission meeting"*, Broschure MNH/NAM/99.2, Brussels: World Health Organization 1999, p. 9)

Zeldin, S. (2004), Preventing youth violence through the promotion of community engagement and membership, Journal of Community Psychology, Volume 32, Issue 5, Pages 623 - 641, Special Issue: Community Violence . Issue Edited by Mark I. Singer, Daniel J. Flannery. Published Online: 3 Aug 2004

References Cited (as of 1-25-2010)

Anon. Youth Violence: A Report of the Surgeon General - Chapter 4. http://www.surgeongeneral.gov/library/youthviolence/chapter4/sec3.html.

Bandura, A. 1999. Moral disengagement in the perpetration of inhumanities. *Personality and social psychology review* 3, no. 3: 193.

Berkowitz, L. 1989. Frustration-aggression hypothesis: Examination and reformulation. *Psychological Bulletin* 106, no. 1: 59-73.

Dollard, J., L. W. Dobb, N. E. Miller, O. H. Mowrer, and R. R. Sears. 1944. *Frustration and aggression*. K. Paul, Trench, Trubner & co., ltd.

Drexler, M. 2007. How racism hurts–literally. *The Boston Globe*, July 15.

Gover, Kevin. 2000. Remarks at the Ceremony Acknowledging the 175th Anniversary of the Establishment of the Bureau of Indian Affairs. *American Indian Law Review* 25, no. 1: 161-163.

Kilpatrick, D. G., K. J. Ruggiero, R. Acierno, B. E. Saunders, H. S. Resnick, and C. L. Best. 2003. Violence and risk of PTSD, major depression, substance abuse/dependence, and comorbidity: Results from the National Survey of Adolescents. *Journal of Consulting and Clinical Psychology* 71, no. 4: 692-699.

Kruk, M. R., J. Halasz, W. Meelis, and J. Haller. 2004. Fast positive feedback between the adrenocortical stress response and a brain mechanism involved in aggressive behavior. *Behavioral Neuroscience* 118: 1062-1070.

Langston, Mike. 2003. Addressing the Need for a Uniform Definition of Gang-Involved Crime. *FBI Law Enforcement Bulletin* 72, no. 2 (February). http://www.fbi.gov/publications/leb/2003/feb03leb.pdf.

Maslow, A. H. 1943. A theory of human motivation. *Psychological review* 50, no. 4: 370-396.

Miller, N. E. 1941. I. The frustration-aggression hypothesis. *Psychological Review* 48, no. 4: 337-342.

Montagu, Ashley. 2008. *Man's Most Dangerous Myth: The Fallacy Of Race*. Whitley Press, November 4.

National Institute of Health. Genome.gov | Epigenomics Fact Sheet. *National Human Genome Research Institute*. http://www.genome.gov/27532724.

Office of Juvenile Justice and Delinquency Prevention. 1999. 1996 National Youth Gang Survey. *1996 National Youth Gang Survey*. July. http://ojjdp.ncjrs.gov/pubs/96natyouthgangsrvy/contents.html.

Office of the Surgeon General. 2001. *Youth Violence: A Report of the Surgeon General*. U.S. Department of Health & Human Services, January. http://www.surgeongeneral.gov/library/youthviolence/chapter1/sec1.html#intro.

Anderson, Jack. 2001. Meridian Magazine - Ideas and Society, Lucifer on the Loose. http://www.meridianmagazine.com/ideas/990430looselucifer.html.

Council of National Psychological Associations for the Advancement of Ethnic Minority Interests. 2003. *Psychological Treatmentof Ethnic Minority Populations*. Washington, D.C.: Association of Black Psychologists, November. http://www.apa.org/pi/oema/resources/brochures/treatment-minority.pdf.

Iwamasa, Gayle Y. 2003. Recommendations for the Treatment of Asian America/Pacific Islander Populations. *Psychological Treatment of Ethnic Minority Populations* (November): 34.

Meyers, Linda James Myers,, Anthony Young, Ezemenari Obasi, and Suzette Speight. 2003. Chapter 3: Rececommendations for the Psychological Treatment of Persons of African Descent. In *Psychological Treatment of Ethnic Minority Populations*, 34. Washington, D.C.,: Association of Black Psychologists, November.

Brave Heart, Maria Yellow Horse. 2003. The historical trauma response among natives and its relationship with substance abuse: A Lakota illustration. *Journal of Psychoactive Drugs* 35, no. 1: 7-13.

Walters, K. L., and J. M. Simoni. 2002. Reconceptualizing Native women's health: an" indigenist" stress-coping model. *American Journal of Public Health* 92, no. 4: 520.

www.ingramcontent.com/pod-product-compliance
Lightning Source LLC
Chambersburg PA
CBHW072234270326
41930CB00010B/2123

* 9 7 8 0 9 8 3 5 9 8 8 0 0 *